WHAT A HOOT! LET'S RECRUIT!

JEFFREY S JENSEN

Jensen, Jeffrey, 1956-

What A Hoot! Let's Recruit!: Business development tactics for making your company the best in your industry / by Jeffrey Jensen.

p. cm.

Hard Cover ISBN: 978-1-940984-6 4-3

Library of Congress Control Number: 2014917734

Self-actualization (Psychology). 2. Job Satisfaction. 3. Success. 4.

BF000.000000 2013

650.1 – dc22

Printed in the United States of America.

10 9 8 7 6 5 4 3 2 1

GRATITUDE

To my wife, Taryn, who has been at the heart of our young men's compassion, kindness, and respect of life. Thank you for being so supportive of me in my many endeavors over the years!

I appreciate you more than you know. You have supported me through the good and the bad times that settle on everyone's doorsteps.

You are loved by myself and many!

To my children, Jason, Landon, and Brady: You have been the reason why I try to achieve in my own life—to set a great example for you and your children. This book is written for you. I hope that long after my time, you and your children will benefit from the encouraging principles included in What a Hoot! Let's Recruit!

The three of you are loved beyond compare!

To my parents, Lawrence and Gwen Jensen: You are the best parents a son could ask for. The core values I have today are because of the both of you. Thank you for your encouragement and support throughout my entire life; they are instilled in the way I move through the world.

From you, I learned a great work ethic, a foundation of faith, and a spirit of doing the right thing ALWAYS!

I love you both!

To the people who have invested their hard-earned money in purchasing this book. You have put me in a privileged position to share my experiences and the benefits of recruiting really well. I hope in these pages you find great ideas you can put to use immediately, and that you will share with me the benefits you experience from what you have learned in What a Hoot! Let's Recruit!

To your success!

ACKNOWLEDGMENTS

I would like to recognize and thank the following people for their support, encouragement, and expertise in helping me get *What a Hoot! Let's Recruit!* to the people it will benefit most. I would also like to thank those who continue to book me for speaking engagements so I may spread the word about recruiting effectively. Special thanks goes to:

Ken Allen, Joe Cucchiara, Ray Eickhoff, Claudia Fast, Susan Friedmann, Liz Gregersen, Daniel Harkavy, Tony Hseih, Rachel Langaker, Michael J. Maher, John Maxwell, CJ McDaniel, Andrea McNichol, Leo Novsky, Tim Sanders, Shiloh Schroeder, Patrick Snow, Tyler Tichelaar, John Yokoyama.

CONTENTS

FOREWORD

When I bought my first recruiting company at age twenty-six, I had no idea that most of my working life would be centered around recruiting.

Early on, I noticed that some companies just seem to have the right mojo and continue to grow when other companies are a flash in the pan. I also noticed that the companies asking me to assist in their recruiting efforts were willing to make the investment it took to attract and find the right employees to add to their companies. I have always made it a habit to hang out with and engage people who are older or more experienced than me so I can gain knowledge of what really works and what is fodder. The common thread I have discovered among outstandingly successful people I have met and read about is that they have remained hungry. They are hungry for education, opportunity, contacts, growth, balance, and fulfillment. To that end, they are more positive and focused on making great use of each and every day they are given because they realize each day is such a gift.

Successful people continue to execute their plans every day. They know that every day they are not moving ahead, they are falling behind. They take responsibility for their successes, and yes, for their failures. Most are of the opinion that you can't have success without failure. Failure is embraced by those who are on the path to executing their plans. I will share some failures throughout the book to save you some time and keep you directed to quicker results with your efforts. Yes, some of those failures are my own. Hopefully, my failures will help you succeed. I can promise you that if you truly take to heart the disciplines, suggestions, and anecdotes shared with you in this book, you will achieve the success you are looking for in your recruiting efforts.

In *What A Hoot! Let's Recruit!* you will learn lifelong skills not only for successfully recruiting but in all aspects of your career and your life. My hope is that you will be encouraged not to listen to others around you who question you about achieving your goals. Do not let others, who don't support and encourage you to be your best, to dampen your goals. Following their lead will only make you common. Don't consider what others might think of your aspirations. Only you know the tiger that churns in your head and heart.

My goal in writing this book has been to make recruiting for you a "hoot!" I want you to be invigorated and challenged in your quest to find the best, hire the best, and retain the best people in your industry.

Everyone is responsible for creating his or her own luck. I wish you the best of luck as you create momentum and ignite synergy toward your growth in the recruiting spectrum.

To your success,

Jeff Jensen

Jeff Jensen

INTRODUCTION

No company or organization lasts forever. Not one! Some get acquired by larger concerns; some lose their grips on a unique benefit proposition; others have obvious leadership dysfunctions, or they may fail to maintain a profit in challenging times; some are even traced back to a series of bad hires.

Your future is coming—like it or not. If you find a good employee, how will you truly know whether he will be a long-term great find or just another bad hire? Your future is being written this very day, based on the poor or great choices you make going forward in relation to recruiting for your company or organization. I bet you would like to know how to find the great hires?

Are you fed up with bad hires costing you time, money, and valuable resources? If you have good team members now and you need more like them, do you know how and where to find them? Does someone out there have proven time-tested principles that can consistently work for you? Can you take another year of the same people doing the same thing with the same results? Will this be another year of recruiting experimental prospects and hoping and praying that they work out?

I know the pain of landing a great hire only to have the competition move in and steal your hard-earned employee away. Or you train, invest, entertain, and pour your energy into an employee, only to have her quit. That is not a proud or inspirational moment in a leader's life. Nor does it feel good to bring a new employee on to your team only to discover she doesn't have the capacity to perform well in the position for which you hired her. Oops, my bad!

If you knew where to find the great hires, would that save you some anxiety? Would you like to learn what attracts the right people to your company? Would you like to know how to retain the *great* hires you make? If you could duplicate the process again and again, would that benefit you and your company? Do you think more people will come to work for your company if they know other superstars are there?

I am looking forward to sharing with you some of my thirty years of recruiting experience in a variety of industries. My experiences range from being President of the Knapp Agency (a management and staffing placement company) and President of the Lynnwood Placement Center, Inc. (a logging placement company), to Chairman of the Lynn-O-Rama Festival (a not-for-profit city festival in Lynnwood, Washington) and President of the Seattle Mortgage Bankers Association (a professional membership association). Some of the examples I will share with you include taking a non-profit association to a 32 percent gain in membership in a single year, a mortgage office gaining a 71 percent increase in personnel in an economically challenged year, and a successful statewide recruiting legislative initiative that created a great attractant. *What a Hoot! Let's Recruit!* produces results and offers up more ideas to you than any one company could possibly execute. You will find in these pages at least one great idea that, if you apply it really well, will empower you to succeed in your recruiting efforts to grow your company or organization.

I hear it all the time: "Recruiting is hard." "I just haven't had any success with recruiting." "Can't I hire somebody to do the recruiting?" "I don't want to make another bad hire."

You are not alone, my friend. If you are reading this book, you are probably looking to get better at what you do and how you do it. Your actions and how you present yourself to your environment will determine for both you and your company whether you will exist marginally or experience a gratifying, refreshing, and revitalizing life of significance.

I want to be your coach, mentor, and accountability partner— whatever it takes—to help you become more successful at the challenge of recruiting. Mark this book up, flag it, bend the pages at the corners, highlight passages, do whatever it takes to make this a tool you use daily and refer to often. What I really am hoping for is to hear back from you on which ideas you put your own special twist to that blossomed into a really big win for you and your company.

As a recruiter, you are not only promoting your company—you are promoting yourself. If you are in a position of recruiting for a company, you may not necessarily be labeled with the job title of recruiter. You could be a CEO, Owner, Executive V.P., National or Regional Director, HR person, Manager, Business Development person, Talent Acquisition Manager…and so on. In any case, someone has believed in you enough to trust your judgment and selected you as the best person to grow and strengthen your company. You are the chosen one to get the message out about your culture and brand. Own it, enjoy it, and have fun with it. Your attitude will be contagious.

If you are ready to accept the challenges, I am looking forward to going on this journey with you.

CHAPTER 1

OMG!
THIS IS SO EASY...

"Some people want it to happen,
Some wish it would happen,
Others make it happen."

— Michael Jordan

One of the first things you want to do to begin recruiting quality employees is to establish what it is you want to do with your company or organization. What is your culture? As you lead, where are you going? Whom do you need to get you there?

In this book, you will learn the steps that will help you to answer those questions and the techniques to help you get what you want. Please understand that no company will be able to engage all of the techniques you are about to learn in this book. I have accumulated some really great techniques that have worked well over my thirty years of recruiting experience. This experience has come through trial and error of concepts, marketing experiments, and different mousetraps that have proven themselves over time. Hats off to you if you are able to implement a majority of the techniques in this book, but if you get really good with just a few that fit your culture, you will have unbridled success in your recruiting efforts.

YOUR CULTURE IS YOUR BRAND

So how do you get started in defining your culture? That begins with you! Great leaders seek out other great leaders. They realize that no one person can do everything on his or her own. Through group collaboration, real success comes to life. A strong culture has to start with you! Embedding solid principles and practices that will withstand diversity and distractions may, at times, be out of your control. Too many changes in a company's culture year after year will cause you to lose momentum. We will identify a timeframe together later in this chapter that can work for you as a basis to apply your culture.

Culture is the sum result of the **vision + mission + core values** that you and your company's leaders create.

These three things must be clearly developed and defined before you can begin to build your culture. The vision is where your company is going, the mission is where your company is today, and your company's purpose and its core values are the best practices and priorities you set in place for everyone to honor.

When you stay focused on defining and clarifying these three components of your culture, you'll find that the culture will begin to develop automatically. By following this upfront plan, you will build a more attractive culture and appeal to the high quality recruits you will be working with yourself. Your selected candidates will bring their high quality friends, and their friends, and their friends. These people will attract high quality clients. Business is easy. Life is good!

If you don't define your culture, your employees will, and that is when the wheels start to come off the bus.

From time to time, some minor tinkering may be required to update your vision + mission + core values to remain a vibrant company. Embrace change. It really is the only constant, so let yourself get comfortable and roll with it.

Establishing your company's culture is absolutely essential to a successful recruiting effort for everyone involved. I can't stress enough how imperative it is that the people you are seeking for your company understand your culture. A clear vision must be defined that shows where your company is today and where your company expects to be in the future. That is your first step in defining culture.

Zappos' CEO Tony Hsieh learned early on how critical culture is to attract the right people to your company. Zappos' culture is different in many ways. For example, the company offers a life coach for employees and a library with free books; all new hires train in the call center, no matter what their positions are. After training, they are offered a certain percentage of their salary to quit—just to make sure they are committed to the company. I'm sure, because of the attractive culture Zappos has created, few if any of the new hires take the company up on that offer.

Let's get started with your culture.

VISION

The first component of developing your culture is to establish the vision.

The good news is that creating a vision is a lot easier and less time-consuming than you might think.

For the following exercise, spend no more than thirty minutes to complete your first *draft*.

No matter what device you are using to record the collaboration and brainstorming done in your organization, I've found that by simply entering "draft" at the top of the document, you will receive a lot more input; otherwise, people tend to assume the vision is final, so there's no point in providing any real feedback. Free your mind of everything except past positive achievements that seem at least somewhat relevant to creating a great vision. My past experience has shown that those who just dive in and get ideas flowing almost always are the ones who emerge from this process with the most creative and inspiring visions.

Here are some key questions to get the creative juices flowing:

- What does our organization's brand look like?
- What size is it compared to others in our industry?
- What do we do really well?
- What effect are we having on our clients' lives?
- How do people who work here feel about their jobs?
- How do I, as a leader, feel about our business?

These are just a few suggested questions to help you get going on the visioning process. Once you have completed the visioning process, you will have a clearly articulated path for your organization and something that won't change every time the market or your mindset shifts.

You might include specific contributions that you or your colleagues have made to past successes, or skills, techniques, and resources that could be assets in achieving your vision. Writing down anything good that comes to mind is fine. The idea is just to create a base of positive energy and high-quality experiences on which you can build for future success. The more you focus on the positives, not on the present-day problems, the more likely you are to attain the greatness you envision.

Let's get your BHAGs (Big Hairy Audacious Goals) on! Expand your ideas into something BIG yet specific. Don't worry about the "how" at this point; just put it out there and let's swim to it. If the ideas you are putting out there aren't a little intimidating, then you probably haven't pushed yourself hard enough. Don't be trying to impress other people here. Go with what comes from your gut.

Having gone through this process a number of times, I know that if you take yourself from the present to the future and envision yourself living there, it makes the future a reality for you. You need to taste it, breathe it, and feel it as though you are already living there.

Beleaguering this part of the exercise will take the energy out of the process. Set a boundary around keeping the visioning process to thirty minutes.

We have all popped popcorn. Think of all the noise and energy in that short process and then how quiet it gets toward the end. That is what you are looking for here. A burst of great ideas and energy all at once will give you a bucketful of options to collaborate on. A day or two before we start the process, I will typically issue some expectations of what we hope to accomplish while we are envisioning the vision. This extra time gives people the opportunity to think about what they might contribute to the exercise.

Here are some examples of vision statements to help you get started:

1. We understand that ours is a business of relationships, so we strive to make every aspect of the customer experience an awesome one.

2. We conduct ourselves with high integrity and total honesty. We will not allow shortcuts.

3. We will strive to be the best versions of ourselves through constant and never-ending improvement.

4. We see the optimum potential in people, not for whom they are, but for whom they can become.

5. We will all help one another...to learn, teach, and share our accomplishments because together, we can reach higher goals individually and as a whole.

6. We show up on time and are respectful of each other's time.

7. We laugh often and enjoy our time together.

8. We will challenge each other to move out of our comfort zones.

9. What you think is what you generate to the world—attitude is everything.

10. We are dedicated to improving the lives of those we work with and others around us.

A great vision is inspiring. It gets you and everyone in the organization excited to come to the project at hand and everyone wants to be involved in it every day to improve on it. Having a vision does not mean dreaming about unrealistic goals. A vision must also be structurally solid. You have to have a real opportunity of achieving this goal, based on where you are right now and where you are trying to go.

Remember, a vision is not a strategic plan. The vision articulates where you, as a group, are going. The plan tells us how we're actually going to get there. Every good plan has a start and finish period established. As a rule of thumb, five years (sixty short months) to establish a timeframe for your vision is a great place to start from. Success needs to be measured. If there are no markers in place, you can't gauge your progress or the lack thereof.

When we do effective visioning, we're moving toward the future we want, not just reacting to a present-day reality we don't like. If we do our job well in this regard, I believe we keep our competitors reacting to what we're doing, instead of the other way around.

A vision also makes it much easier to handle the strategic opportunities that present themselves every day. Your vision will take out the agony over what to do with opportunities that present themselves to your company. Having a vision makes decisions much easier:

The only opportunities even worth considering are those that will help you attain your vision.

Now put the draft aside for a few days. Go back to all the other stuff you do every day. This is where you reach out and get input from people you trust and respect. Those people may include a mentor, peers in the business community, business partners, colleagues, family members, or close friends.

But remember that it's your vision, and you're not obligated to change anything.

After a couple of days when you're ready to revise, have your team meet again and read your draft through from start to finish. This is the time to make the vision more real. Don't delete anything. Copy your original draft. Hopefully, you are a little anxious to execute your vision. Are you inspired? Do you get a charge out of it when you are reading it?

It is now the time to get specific. How specific should you get? Try to avoid vague statements now like "We want to be number one by such and such date." Use real sales numbers that mean something. Without definition, you will have no details on measured success. What are the key financial numbers that define success for you? Sales volume? Market share? Recruitment goals?

Now begin the alignment process by having each partner in the group present his or her draft. Be careful that everyone is clear on both the timeframe (five minutes) and the topic we've chosen. Once each person has put together his or her vision, compare your drafts, listening carefully to what each person has to say, and have someone be responsible for capturing themes on a whiteboard as you go.

Give everyone a chance to weigh in on how strongly he or she feels about each theme. If there are ten themes up on the board, you might give each participant four votes, or something along those lines. The votes help the group get clear on the top-priority items. Remember, there are no right or wrong visions. Then work to identify common themes and come to agreement on a single vision you can all work toward. You will find that employees will hold each other accountable to the vision, and it empowers each member of your company to enforce the vision everyone has helped create.

I have found that most of us work with key managers who are prominent or equal players, so we need to get in alignment with them. Leaders pursuing different visions for the same project will almost always create enormous problems in any organization.

Your work day is short, and time spent agonizing over opportunities that take you away from the vision is a poor use of your time. The preferred path would be working toward the future that everyone has agreed upon, in terms of how it will look. Please make sure you refer to the vision frequently and embrace it. You might even make it a screensaver wallpaper on your company's computers. It shouldn't end up like some business plans that have a lot of energy put into them, but only see the light of day at the beginning and end of the year.

Finally, it's time to share the vision with everyone who will be involved in implementing it. When you roll out your vision to the bigger group, it's inevitable that people will ask questions about how you intend to achieve the vision. They're asking you about the *how*. The vision, however, is the *what*. It's totally fine if you don't know how you're going to get there. Later, you will figure out the *how*.

I frequently use a special technique to expose our culture to a prospect early on in the rubbing noses part of recruiting. I have made it a habit of excusing myself from an interview to make copies of resumes or get water for the interviewee. Before I leave the room, I give a copy of our vision/mission statement to a prospect and ask him to read it while I'm gone and let me know when I return whether he has any questions about who our team is and what our culture is like. That one action alone may have a recruit thinking to himself, "This is the team I want to hang with," or maybe, "This team would expect too much from me." The best thing you can do for yourself or your company is to find out early on whether this culture will be a good strengths fit for both parties before proceeding too far down the path of making a bad hire.

A bad hire can badly hurt your organization, and even, quite literally, cost lives. The logging business at one time was one of the most dangerous professions to be in, and the percentage of on-the-job deaths in that business each year was higher than in any other industry. I never had a placement of mine die on a job where I placed him, but I did have a really uncomfortable experience happen because of a bad hire.

In one instance, I was president of a company in the late '70s that placed loggers in the Northwest and Southeast Alaska. I had placed Ben with a company called Louisiana Pacific. In that position, he was responsible for setting towing lines behind a skidder to tow logs (a choker setter). Louisiana Pacific wanted someone who had the potential to work up to a position that carried more responsibility. I received a call from the show boss (field supervisor) that Ben had left camp and was headed down to see me.

The day before, Ben had gotten angry at the show boss. He had knocked the boss' metal helmet off his head and shot a hole in it with a pistol he was carrying. Ben didn't take well to being told what to do. He left because his rate of pay was $4.00 an hour less than what I had told him it would be when I sent him up from Seattle. The pay was going to be paid back to him retroactively, but he didn't stay around long enough to find that out. Long story short, he never shot a hole in my helmet, but he was a bad hire. In this particular case, a more in depth background check would have saved me some embarrassment.

Defining your culture and finding employees who fit into that culture will help you stay focused on the big picture rather than dealing with employee conflicts and other issues.

MISSION

Mission is the second part of defining your culture. A well thought-out mission statement can provide the focus and motivation you need to take your business to the future you have envisioned. You will want to allow the same time frame as you did for your vision. This is your **why** that will complement your core values, which we will cover next. Your mission statement drives your business' personality. It is where you make your commitment to great customer service and a "Wow" experience for your current and future employees. It is where you commit to offering the marketing support to enforce your branding. Your mission is the soul of your branding. It is the very reason your company does what it does.

Your mission is about getting really clear and laser-focused on your direction. It steers you toward the right customers and the right employees. It is your internal branding. Your mission is something you should write and post in places where every single member of your staff can see it. It should be brought out at your interview with a prospect. As the leader of your company, look at your mission often. If you as a leader keep that mission statement in your office some place where it is easy to see, it will keep you on goal as you are moving through your day and help prevent you from getting distracted by the things that can take you off your mission. Actually time block on your calendar a monthly review of your mission with your group. Are you staying focused on the task at hand? Remind yourself of it. Then live it and breathe it. Every. Single. Day.

When you live your mission, amazing, phenomenal things start to happen. People will spread the word to their friends. Your clients are drawn to you, and so are their friends. People get really excited about what you are doing and who you are doing it for. People will give you great customer feedback on surveys. When you ask clients and new hires for testimonials, they will be more than happy to respond with great reviews. You get more customers, increase revenue, and your business grows in leaps and bounds. Your team is more energized, creative, and joyous than ever before because everyone is in alignment with your **why.**

Whenever I begin to develop a mission statement, I fall back on some key questions that help me build my passion for the creative work we as a group are about to embark on. I have found that these questions elicit and raise my colleagues' passion about what we do. Here are some examples of key questions to get your creative juices stirring:

- If we want to lead and change our industry, do we pick our team to do that?

- How are we helping others by letting them join our company?

- Who is our market?

- Why did we choose this industry?

- How do we help others with the profit we create?

- Can we do things in a different way to improve our clients and employees' lives?

I also have listed a few well-known company mission statements below to help get you started:

- To combine aggressive strategic marketing with quality products and services at competitive prices to provide the best insurance value for consumers. — Aflac

- To discover, develop and deliver innovative medicines that help patients prevail over serious diseases. — Bristol-Myers Squibb Company

- At the heart of The Chevron Way is our Vision to be the global energy company most admired for its people, partnership and performance. — Chevron

- We are a global family with a proud heritage passionately committed to providing personal mobility for people around the world. — Ford Motor Company

- Philanthropy supports the social responsibility cornerstone of Lucent's mission: To live up to our responsibilities to serve and enhance the communities in which we work and live and the society on which we depend. — Lucent Technologies

- To bring inspiration and innovation to every athlete in the world. — Nike

Your mission statement should be the driving force behind everything your team does both within your company and externally with prospects, vendors, customers, and associates. It also shapes your internal corporate culture.

As you create your mission statement, use words that move you and will draw you into action. Drop in words like "passionate," "sensational," "spectacular," "fun," and "marvelous" to add spark to your mission statement. Get really clear about your passion and core values, which we will cover next. Use dynamics, visuals, and acceleration words that inspire you to action. Describe your purpose using defining, colorful verbs and adjectives to "pop" your statements. Keep your mission statement fairly short, and make sure it feels really good when you read and say it. It should be easy to memorize, much like a creed. Create a few succinct sentences that capture the essence of your business' goals and the philosophies underlying them. The mission statement should make totally evident what your business is all about to your customers, employees, and vendors.

When writing a mission statement, I've made it a practice to involve everyone in a leadership role. If people believe in and create the statement as a team, they will support and own it. For the last mission statement I was involved in, I purposely made no comments about the statement but let others create it. Something put together by a single leader in the company is not something the whole team will buy into. If all your team members have some input into your mission statement, they will strive hard to honor its other creators, expecting mutual respect in return for the ideas they offered for it. The mission statement will morph from time to time as the company grows and new objectives become relevant to the company's health.

It is so easy for any business leader to get bogged down in the day-to-day activities of business life. Daily, a distraction or two can quickly take us off course. The beauty comes in recognizing the distraction and staying on mission to move the team to the desired result. Your mission statement continually reminds your team of where you have been, where you are going, what you are doing, and why you are doing it.

The final piece to the puzzle is your core values.

CORE VALUES

This last component of defining your culture will require you to commit to heading a values based company. *Your core values will be more or less permanent for all the future years of your company. Your vision and mission need to remain somewhat flexible from time to time, depending on your growth and the different markets you enter.* Your *personal values* will need to be projected into your business values.

As defined by businessdictionary.com, a core value is "A principle that guide an organization's internal conduct as well as its relationship with the external world. Core values are usually summarized in the mission statement or in a statement of core values." Your core values are what support your vision.

As a leader, living by your company's core values will require you to have maturity. For example, being patient about measuring profit and revenue increases that will pave the road to a values benefit for those looking to join your company.

Living your core values might even involve you completing a lifeline chart. In this exercise, you start with the date of your birth and move from left to right on a median line, capturing the points of impact in your life that formed who you are. You chart the dates progressively, with the highs (being above the median line) and the lows (being below the median line) that resulted in changes in your life and shaped who you are today.

I have done this exercise as a group with those people helping me to create the vision and mission statement. You would be surprised how raw this experience is and how much you find out about the other people you are working with as each creates his or her chart. It is a very healthy exercise for everyone on the team. It isn't something you just read and say, "That's a good idea!" Do it!

On the following page is an example to help you get started on your lifeline.

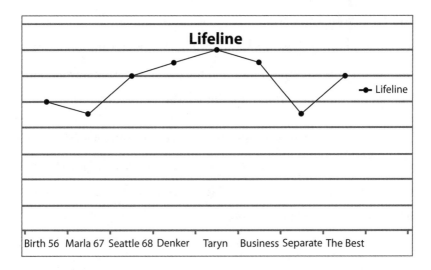

The points on the chart reflect the following key moments in my life:

- I was born in Wichita, Kansas, in 1956.

- My sweet cousin Marla was killed in a bus/train accident in 1967. (I learned to be kind to everyone. You never know how long you have someone.)

- We moved to Seattle from Wichita in 1968. (I learned to take some calculated risks.)

- My Grandpa Denker passed away. He was a role model (mayor, entrepreneur, well-respected).

- I married my high school sweetheart Taryn (beginning of family life).

- I established my first business (creating, growing, success, learning, but didn't stay balanced).

- Taryn and I separated. (Not the best of times, but we learned from it and reunited.)

- The best. (The best years are yet ahead of me.)

You have your own events in your life that shaped who you are today. By sharing those with others and others sharing theirs with you, an understanding is created of the paths you have traveled that have put all of you at that moment on the same path.

The core values express who you are or who you want to be. Each value should be one word or at most a short phrase (but ideally one word) that is significant and meaningful to you personally. This one word or short phrase doesn't have anything to do with the company's values.... Instead, at this point, you will want to mesh people's core values together. From that, you will arrive at agreed upon core values for your organization.

Ask managers to test values with employees and even take a look at exit interview notes of ex-employees.

Think about any employees whom you think represent your company culture well.

Test your commitment here by asking yourself this question: Are you willing to hire/fire people based on whether they fit your core values, even if an employee adds a lot of value in the short term?

Combine people's core values (again). Just have the few people assigned to helping create the core values make the final version. Don't do this by committee; you can't make everyone happy.

Roll out the core values to the entire company. Going forward, integrate core values into everything you do, and specifically, around hiring, firing, and performance reviews.

As with many endeavors of this type, vision statements, mission statements, and core values can often become words on a plaque or fliers on a bulletin board. If you are committed to continually striving toward the culture you are pining for, it is up to you as a leader to lead the effort. You will be pleasantly surprised when you notice daily behaviors and decision making rotating quite naturally and smoothly toward the culture you envisioned. Decision making becomes easier because everyone's expectations are in alignment.

The results of time well spent developing core values will show up in the employees' belief in the established set of core values, their sense of ownership of the values, and their desire to see them "lived out" on a daily basis. Past experience, however, also has shown me that continued work must be done to integrate the core values even further into the organization's foundational elements and to improve individual accountability to behave in accordance with the values.

Lastly, continuous improvement suggestions should be implemented on a quarterly basis as well as discussions being held to gauge the progress of employee involvement and ownership.

The result creates a focus for how your company conducts business, delivers services, and treats individuals, both inside and outside the organization.

Here are some examples of core values to help get you started:

- Commitment to WOW. We create WOW through exemplary service and experience, consistently exceeding the expectations of our customers and team members.

- Admire people.

- Find a better way.

- Be passionate about making a difference.

- We acknowledge that our business' success depends upon every single customer's complete satisfaction.

- Uncompromising integrity. Our character and honor are steadfast. We conduct ourselves in a manner that is beyond reproach.

The basic work and time you have invested at this point sets the foundation for your team's quest to build and grow your business, a quest that will be rewarding for all.

Now that we have gotten the basics out of the way, it is time to move into some of the fun stuff that you get to create to fit your company or organization.

This isn't your typical book. Before we go further, I encourage you to stop right here and get your culture RIGHT. Most books typically go from chapter to chapter and try to keep the reader excited about what will unfold next as the book progresses. Think of *What A Hoot! Let's Recruit!* as more of an app to apply right now. You will be more empowered as you head into the great techniques coming at you if you do the work that needs to be done right here, right now. Communicate to the world about your culture. Don't let people forget about what you do. You need to be continually promoting (not selling) your unique benefit proposition.

Everything hinges upon what you establish in your culture. If you are just going to make this another read, then I have failed in my intent to make you better at recruiting. After you have completed this most essential element on your way to success, please proceed with the rest of this book.

CHALLENGE

Write down five things that would attract you to a company that are non-negotiable items for you. Would these five things be the premise for helping you to get started on identifying your culture?

1. _____

2. _____

3. _____

4. _____

5. _____

CHAPTER 2

CREATING THE ATTRACTANT

"Would you work with you?"

— Anonymous

IDENTIFYING WHAT ATTRACTS PEOPLE TO YOUR COMPANY

Do you promote work/life balance? Are you sincere? Is your company's senior leadership sincere? Do *you* attract people to your company?

The best way to begin to find out where your company is at is to learn everything about your industry that you can. Read publications produced by people in your industry. Be the expert. Improve your confidence with the knowledge base you continue to build. Be voracious in your reading habits and by listening to CDs that push new ideas. Have a thirst for knowledge. Show people that *you* are on top of your game by your knowledge base being so expansive. It is eye-opening and fun to have the ideas of so many fascinating and successful people pouring into your own success as that continues to increase. Those who are wise enough to stop, listen, and read will have that separating edge that brings success.

Do you know what appeals to the five generations of potential talent out there? What will make them attracted (or not) to your company?

By the five generations, I mean the Traditionalists (born 1929-1946), Baby Boomers (born 1947-1965), Generation X (born 1966-1979), the Millennials (born 1980-1994), and Generation Z (born 1994-present).

TRADITIONALISTS

There are 27 million of them out there, and approximately 6 million of them are currently employed. They are the smallest group in the workforce. They have a strong sense of duty and sacrifice, a respect for authority, and trust in the government. They value accountability and have a strong work ethic. They believe promotions and recognition come with job tenure. They are the mothers and fathers of the Baby Boomers. Many of them lived through the Great Depression and World War II. Most Traditionalists have a predominant trait of being very conservative with monetary concerns.

A few Traditionalists you may know are: Alan Greenspan, Marilyn Monroe, Martin Luther King, Jr., Gloria Steinem, Robert F. Kennedy, Barbara Walters, and Elvis Presley.

BABY BOOMERS

They are the largest workforce out there at the writing of this book. There are 76 million of them and 55 million of them are currently employed. I am one of the 55 million. We are of a mindset to question authority. We pursue capitalist opportunities for financial success. We are of a free spirit, equal rights, prosperous times, and relationship-oriented mindset. We live to work and don't take enough time off to play. We preach balance in home and work and don't do that very well. We can work within a team environment very well, and we enjoy collaborative input to expose solutions to problems. We love to share new ideas with subordinates to see them excel; that brings satisfaction for us. We love to learn and stay on the cutting edge of advancements. We love to compete and have the appropriate tools to be successful. Give us a problem and point us in the right direction and we will do our best to complete the objective.

Baby Boomers typically have not really experienced financial woes on a large scale as a group. Even with the recent recession, Baby Boomers still control nearly 70 percent of the total net worth of American households and own 80 percent of all the money in savings and loan associations.

Bill Gates, Donald Trump, Princess Diana, Richard Branson, Laura Bush, Jeff Bezos, Ann Coulter, and Oprah Winfrey are all Baby Boomers.

GEN-XERS

They are the next largest group of people coming at you in the workforce. There are 60 million of them moving about the face of the earth, and 45 million of them are currently employed.

Gen-Xers have had more free time growing up than the previous two identifiable groups. That has resulted in making them more self-reliant. That is why they cherish their personal time as adults. They question authority just as their parents, the Baby Boomers, did. They don't feel the loyalty to an employer that the Traditionalists do. They are a bit more cynical than the Traditionalists and Baby Boomers. Gen-Xers focus on how they can advance in their careers and develop their skills. They don't get stuck in process and pine toward the outcome. They love open communication; in fact, they demand it. They don't accept policies and procedures without getting to the bottom of why these things exist and whether they are reasonable.

If you explain how their efforts contribute to the company's success, they are totally on board. They want to be challenged and not do redundant tasks. They like to learn. If you align with them in a way that creates ownership from them, they love that. If you focus on results and allow flexibility on time frames, they will be in their strengths curve.

A few famous Gen-Xers you may know are: Marisa Mayer, Tiger Woods, Adam Sandler, Tony Hawk, Mariah Carey, and Jennifer Capriati.

MILLENNIALS

Recently, the Millennials have created a whole new dynamic in the workforce. I love this group! My three boys are in this group. They bring youthful exuberance and great energy to their environment. They are the smallest group with 32 million currently employed and a total count of 88 million. Obviously, the employed number will continue to grow within this group. Millennials had lots of things to keep them busy while growing up. The Internet, social networks, ESPN, CNN, FOX, travel flexibility, more efficient automobiles with GPS's, laptops, and smartphones.

The Millennials respond to being recognized many times each day. People who are already working with you or from the same generation I am (Baby Boomers) might see such repetitive reinforcement as a self-serving unrealistic showering of over-indulgence. However, the workplace culture has shifted dramatically in the last few years. To attract and engage the Millennials, your company recognition platform needs to be well done. It makes a difference to them what they are recognized for, how they are being recognized, and how often they are being recognized.

The youngest generation is always driving and aligning with changes while keeping a watchful eye on its predecessors' errors and working toward avoiding the same errors in the workplace.

A little side note: Millennial men tend to make more money and be more satisfied with their current careers than their female counterparts. Millennial men also tend to like beer. At the writing of this book, Heineken is their favorite. Millennials will maintain a relationship with a brand as long as they continue to receive functional and emotional benefits. Major brands are staying relevant with Millennials while staying true to what made them great.

Because of all the technology Millennials have had at their fingertips for most of their lives, they communicate frequently. They are responsible for trending on Twitter. You need to know what that is. They are responsible for flash mobs. You need to know what that is.

Some etiquette issues between Millennials and earlier generations are still being figured out, such as: turning off your phone in a meeting, not texting while driving, and being distracted by chirps, beeps, buzzes, bleeps, and tweets.

When attracting and retaining this growing group, you will need to have a great communicative platform with lots of collaboration and positive feedback. They are the "Lone Rangers." By that, I mean they are independent. The men tend to eat and travel alone. The women not so much. Don't shotgun or broad target this group. Focus on them as individuals.

"Communicate, Communicate, Communicate" is what Millennials thrive on. Partner them up with Baby Boomers and both parties will be in their strengths curves. Millennials love to volunteer if they know there is an opportunity to effect change. When you share benefits about your company with Millennials, realize they will be drawn to what your company is doing in the community and the opportunities that might possibly be presented to them to participate. Being actively involved in community events promotes your brand and amplifies your culture to others so find ways to encourage Millennials in this interest.

Don't forget to have frequent achievement recognition moments. Your onboarding and training opportunities need to be fully encompassing and expose developmental opportunities to employees.

Not only Millennials, but almost everyone appreciates recognition of his or her birthday. Providing that recognition is a no brainer. Be creative here. This is a "not to be missed" opportunity.

Your goal as a recruiter, manager, or owner is to understand how this fascinating mix of generations can engage as a team and create not just a good company but a great one.

Having a clear and concise set of job descriptions available to a prospect immediately lets her know what is expected of her and also lets her know as she is evaluating your company whether the bar is set high enough for what she expects from a great company. A clear job description will also allow a candidate to eliminate herself early on from the rubbing noses process if she knows she can't possibly conform to the company's expectations.

A few famous Millennials you may know are: Mark Zuckerberg, Carrie Underwood, Prince William, Serena Williams, and LeBron James.

GENERATION Z OR DIGITAL NATIVES

This generation is born after 1994. Generation Z is on its way to the workforce. At last count, they are 23 million and still growing. They are already exhibiting characteristics of being highly connected to the use of communications. They thrive in acceleration and next, next, next. They will be under a lot of pressure to succeed. They witnessed the Great Recession, the devastation of Katrina, and knew something about Facebook being launched in 2004. It will be interesting to see more of their characteristics evolve as they become more entrenched in the workforce.

Generation Z members you may know include: Ella Marija Lani Yelich-O'Connor (Lorde), Brooklyn Beckham, Apple Martin, Blue Ivy Carter, and Suri Cruise.

RECRUITING THE GENERATIONS

We will cover employee retention in Chapter 8. Just know that over the next few years, while Baby Boomers continue to retire, the upcoming Generation X that is shy of the Baby Boomers by 10 million souls will be the workforce that is available for work. Quite simply, there will be fewer people available for work. By getting better at recruiting, you will be exposing yourself to the best talent available in a shrinking talent pool.

If you are a young recruiter yourself just getting into the business of recruiting, I would like to share a quick story with you. When I was a young recruiter in my twenties, I owned my first company called the Knapp Agency in downtown Seattle. At the time, I had a baby face and looked younger than I was. I remember wanting to put a little gray in my hair to give me more credibility with the older people I was assisting to find jobs.

We had a candidate (who was in his forties, as were most of the people we were placing at that time) whom one of my associates had placed with one of our employer clients. Bob was hired by one of our employer clients, and he had come back to my company to negotiate the placement fee he had agreed to pay upon being hired. My receptionist buzzed me on the phone, explained the situation to me, and asked whether I was free to speak with Bob. I said I was and to have him come back to my office. After I greeted Bob at my office door, he began to chuckle a bit.

Bob asked whether he could speak with the owner. I responded with "I am the owner" and asked him to have a seat. Bob now started to giggle a bit more. He said he was sorry to be giggling, but he explained, "You're young enough to be one of my kids." Being younger and feeling pretty self-important, I was embarrassed by the comment.

To make a long story short, Bob was satisfied with the arrangement we came to regarding the fee he was to pay, and he thanked me for my professionalism. I found that by being humble through the course of the conversation and respecting Bob's view of what he felt was fair for our fee, Bob walked out of my company with a "WOW" experience he could share with his friends and fellow workers. Because I visibly recognized the person sitting before me had double the life experience I had at that time, I gained Bob's trust and gained a little more credibility.

Being younger in this business of recruiting sometimes means it takes a little time to gain people's respect and create credibility for yourself. Keep reading—some great tips are ahead that will save you some time going through the school of hard knocks.

GAME CHANGER

For some of you, what I am going to ask you to do next is going to make you uncomfortable. You need to be *disruptive* in your industry. You need to be the person whom people look to as the game changer. Is your future bright? Is your company's future bright? Can you convey that bright future to the prospects you meet? Do you feel empowered to make a difference in people's lives?

Get it known out there in your industry that you do team building events like indoor skydiving, ropes courses, self-improvement seminars, retreats, president's clubs, birthday celebrations, month-end Mexican fiestas, boat excursions to watch the Blue Angels together, crazy-themed dress-up days, wine tasting events, a day at the races (horses, cars, airplanes, tricycles, babies, whatever!), and philanthropic initiatives. Bring a masseuse into the office for the afternoon to massage those tense and anxious muscles. Let people know you celebrate together!

You want people talking about you and your company in a good way. Being common isn't any fun, and it sure isn't going to attract people who are looking for growth and opportunities.

TELL YOUR STORY

Understand your own authentic story; then articulate it. People don't like to be sold. Today, selling has a negative context, but people respond to a good story they can align with; they will even take up the cause if it captures their imaginations.

This story could be about an employee at your company, about you, about the company itself, about a positive experience that a client had with your company, or a "raving fan" experience.

I've written this book because I am passionate about opportunities that can change people's lives. I have been fortunate enough to be in a position of knowing the needs of my organization and having the skill set to find the people who can benefit it and its employees. I have seen people come from a place of being poor to a place of significance within an organization and then "pay it back" in a way that benefits people because of their newfound options. To watch people perpetuate a good thing is *so* rewarding. Here are just a few examples I've experienced myself:

- I have been involved with chairing a city festival that brought newfound energy to the citizens of that city. Getting the right people in the right positions made all the difference.

- I have been involved in placing people in an organization at a mid-level position and seeing them later become senior executive leaders in those organizations.

- I have been involved in building new homes for people who survived the Hurricane Katrina disaster, so I know what having the right people in place did for those deserving families.

- I have networked to introduce one person to another who could satisfy that first person's lifelong goal.

However, to attract and recruit people to create these opportunities—before there can even be a platform for discussion—the basics have to be addressed.

Obviously, compensation is a key piece of the equation when prospects consider your company.

Your compensation schedule will bring a sense of fairness to a potential prospect. If an incoming employee knows he has the exact same opportunity to be as or more successful than your current top producer on a level playing field, he will likely find that enticing. If someone feels, however, that she may not be getting the same compensation as another employee, that just creates dissension, animosity, and mistrust of the company itself.

Broadcast that you do things like paying for an employee's dry cleaning for the month if he produces the most employer referral calls. Promote the team building events you do. Announce the recognition programs you have. Amplify your compensation program for both originators and staff.

Remember not to make your awards always centered on production. That only creates resentment and animosity with your great medium producers. Instead, make your awards about disciplines or behaviors that you are trying to encourage. This will make your team stronger and more cohesive.

A-players don't have to or want to play with a bunch of C-players. As you continue to build your A-team, you will find that they perpetuate each other. Life is good!

Rave about your origination system. Millennials and Gen-Xers love to know what kind of new toy you have to drive that will be a big part of their daily routine. For the Traditionalists and Baby Boomers, that new toy is not as important. Your top originators and managers are searching for robust all-in-one origination systems that include file status, processing, underwriting, document drawing processes, updates, communication through the operating system, product guideline look-ups, reports generation, interfaces with your contact management database, automatic alerts on compliance dates, and the ability to order from vendors out of one LOS (Loan Operating System) platform. If you want to attract the *best*, the investment in a robust LOS platform will pay you back tenfold when word gets out that you have the most efficient origination system. Outdated or clunky Loan Operating Systems are a deterrent.

I am going to list over fifty event ideas below. Pick one or two or more for your company. Make it a hoot! This can be your signature event that helps define your company's culture. Here is where you can pull out your highlighter and dedicate yourself to items you will implement in your company.

Here we go!

1. An educational reimbursement program that allows employees to choose what they'd like to spend time educating themselves on and offers full flexibility. Some have taken classes in comedy, cooking, public speaking, hot yoga, or dance!

2. Paid time off—forty hours' worth to spend working with a non-profit organization of their choice.

3. Pre-paid bus passes.

4. Pet insurance.

5. Life coach, sales coach, speech coach for one year.

6. Gratuitous sports team tickets to share with clients, friends, and family.

7. Gym, tennis, cycling, golf club memberships.

8. End of the month closing celebrations with a theme: Mexican, Trekkies, Hobbits, Western, Halloween in March, Who am I? Whatever!

9. Free trip to Mexico for you and your spouse, based on goals attained.

10. Certificate or prevalent mug with employee's name on it for "I noticed you doing _____well."

11. Funding a department's marketing account for a great month.

12. Free Parking or the coveted reserved spot in the parking lot for the month.

13. Free game room with a stocked kitchen. Ping Pong anyone?

14. Lockers with showers for the health nuts we all love to hire.

15. Annual Christmas party.

16. One paid personal holiday annually.

17. Espresso for everyone on no particular day or for no particular occasion.

18. Employee assistance or employee concierge programs.

19. After hours, company sponsored events: movie outings, iFly Indoor Skydiving, picnics, softball teams, and other team sports. Even employee golf tourneys.

20. Trivia Thursdays with a free cup of joe to the winner.

21. Company sponsored charity events.

22. A one month sabbatical for every four years of service.

23. An associate discount program to include store discounts, rebate programs with local businesses, travel, entertainment, and merchandise.

24. A catered formal dinner at your business facility for no good reason.

25. A pre-tax dependent care reimbursement plan for both minor and adult care dependents.

26. Employee stock purchase program.

27. Remote options to work from home or abroad.

28. 401ks with a generous employee match program.

29. President's club award trips and dinners.

30. Every five years, employees receive $800 toward a new headset, computer gadget, personal printer, or something techie!

31. Free breakfast on Wednesdays from 7:30 to 8:00 a.m.

32. First day of employment, new hires receive a $250 travel voucher.

33. Paid for late afternoon ski trips with bus service to the mountains while singing the *Gilligan's Island* theme song.

34. Monetary incentives to join and contribute to local industry associations.

35. A gifted Passport Unlimited card to use not only for restaurant services but discounts on merchandise items.

36. Company paid massages on site.

37. Bring in an in office or parking lot rock wall.

38. Barber or salon services on site.

39. Movie day as part of an extended lunch.

40. A quarterly one hour uninterrupted session with the CEO of the company to discuss suggestions for improvements to the company, fishing, the business, vision for the company, the weather.

41. Buy pizza for everyone who stays from 6:00 to 7:30 p.m. for dialing for dollars calls, executing sales scripts, and business development.

42. Offer $500 to the person this week who refers a recruit whom you end up hiring.

43. Scholarship programs for student employees or the sons and daughters of your employees.

44. Casual dress codes on Fridays.

45. Add an additional week of sick leave after five years.

46. Birthday car detailing or birthday spa day.

47. Do a birthday "wheel of fortune" complete with gift cards to local restaurants and businesses.

48. Free smart identity fraud services.

49. Discounted cell services as a result of volume discount for your company.

50. Music playing in the office to complement your environment. For some Baby Boomers, that might be a little Grand Funk Railroad.

51. Bring your dog/cat/bird/lion to work day. Probably best to keep same species coming in on the same day. Limit of eight animals in the house at one time, no barkers, and allow time for animal potty breaks. Maybe have a wall of fame for pets.

52. Lunch with your new employee's direct report a week after the onboarding process to discuss his or her experience and whether he or she felt anything was overlooked.

53. Purchasing a new suit for him or a new outfit for her with a haberdasher coming on site to measure and prepare delivery of the garment.

54. Company paid for sales events in Palm Desert, Florida, Texas, and other destination spots.

55. Incent your employees to assist in recruiting like a "pack of wolves."

LOCATION

It's always beat into everyone's head: Location, location, location. But have you really thought about your current location being conducive to business? Is your location easy for future employees to access? How about access for your clients, vendors, suppliers, etc.? Are the surrounding neighborhoods attractive to your potential employees? You may have to make some hard choices in order to grow. Changing location is never inexpensive, but it may be a necessary move to perpetuate your growth and make your company more attractive.

Place your company in the right region. A lot of times, the specific area to be located is not a mystery; it is probably very evident where your business is coming from, and at times from the urging of your business base, it becomes very apparent where you need to have a presence. At times, different factors change in a particular industry that make it less profitable to stay where you are. Or maybe the industry has moved to a different region because of local restrictions, business saturation, or economic changes that don't make it conducive to conduct your business in the present location any longer. "Move that bus!"

CYA (COVERING YOUR ASSETS)

Periodically, I have initiated a policy with some prospects whom we are in a stiff competition for, to capture the signing of a "Confidentiality Agreement."

The spirit of the "Confidentiality Agreement" is for the prospective employee not to reveal information that he or she may acquire while considering working for you. It can also be damaging once the employee is hired for him to share with current employees the benefits and compensation offer he may have received since it may be slightly different from ones other employees received when they were hired.

In the highly competitive environment of making offers that are attractive to a prospect, it can be a real deflator to have someone going out sharing all of your enticements to the competition. After you have done all of your fact finding, information acquisition from your department heads, and your negotiations (we'll go deeper into this topic in Chapter 7), to have your prospect walk across the street and share all of your work with another company he plans to work for is not a happy moment.

In confidentiality agreements, I have included verbiage that states our offer is null and void if the prospect shares or discusses it with anyone other than a spouse. In certain cases, a prospect may identify a mentor, coach, or family member who is leaned on for advice, so that is acceptable. You can develop a document that is more suited to your style and culture. Although these agreements are not always enforceable if a prospect were to share the terms of your offer with the competition, his or her behavior would speak loudly to the integrity of the individual who signed your agreement. Next!

CHALLENGE

Wouldn't it be easier to recruit if you knew what your prospects were looking for based on their generation characteristics? Are there five characteristics your company has that would help you assess strengths that would allow a particular generation to find great success with your company? If so, write them down. If not, write what you think they should be.

1. _____

2. _____

3. _____

4. _____

5. _____

CHAPTER 3

IF I BUILD A BETTER ME

"Make the most of yourself...for that is all there is of you."

— **Ralph Waldo Emerson**

ALL companies small and large eventually come and go. That is the natural evolution of business.

Many times I have been inspired by people who faced and overcame what seemed like insurmountable odds. They have great stories to tell as a result.

Here is a quote I love from Douglas Conant (Former President/CEO of the Campbell Soup Company):

"Even a brief interaction can change the way people think about themselves, their leaders, and the future. Each of those many connections you make has the potential to become a high point or a low point in someone's day."

As *you* continue to grow your company, keep in mind that *you* need to continue to grow. Be voracious in your appetite to acquire more knowledge of your industry and to improve yourself. Learn and grow from your mistakes.

If you do a gut check, are you optimistic, positive, and influential?

Optimism is contagious and creates a support atmosphere that draws people like bugs to light. It is an attractant. Being positive is critical in your life as well as your recruiting success. Influence comes with being optimistic and positive. People want to be around people who have great stories to tell. People want to be around a positive role model who has persevered despite insurmountable odds. Everyone is drawn to a story he can see himself living.

Always do the right thing. Your character is an attractant. When no one is watching, what decision will you make? Remember in Chapter 1 when we were laying out the architecture for developing culture. One of the biggest influences on company culture is how the senior leadership behaves. As a leader, you are being watched by subordinates, peers, and your friends. The tone of the staff and even the customers reflects directly off of your leadership. If you're not careful, you can, unknowingly, perpetuate an environment of fear and bullying or just dissatisfaction.

When confronting employees about misbehavior and why they felt it would be condoned, be careful that the misbehavior is not a reflection of you or your leadership team. It is up to you to model and be the poster child for ethical behavior. Aspiring to be the role model, following the rules, and walking the talk is a great attractant. People will look to you and your senior leadership team for models of how to behave. They will feel what made you successful might rub off on them if they duplicate behavior.

For instance, someone who holds in his anger when triggered and responds in a respectful manner will set the expectation for others to aspire to. We all know that holding in your anger just isn't that easy at times. Exhibiting and encouraging people to feel free to take a stand and speak their minds leads to diversity and healthy debate, which are signatures of a high performance workplace team. Leading with a tyrannical or an excessively tough style will interfere with your desire to be transparent with your people, and eventually, it will cause resentment, which will negatively affect any initiatives you are trying to launch.

If you continue to earn a reputation of fairness with your people, you will find that justice matters a great deal to them.

As hard as it is, remain global in your thinking; otherwise, it is easy to get caught up in the minutia of tasks that drain your energy. Anything and everything that can be delegated to someone else that takes you away from recruiting activities should be delegated. Spend your time on the "big" picture of growth. Ask yourself, "What is the 40,000-foot view of where we are and where we are going? Am I staying dedicated to vision? What is impeding my ability to get to the markers I established for the controlled growth I am leading?" Then do whatever you need to do to remove those impediments so you can stay focused on your goal.

In the next chapter, I go into more detail about throwing yourself into the humanity stream and being very relationship-oriented through networking. When you are running into obstacles, you need to draw on your relationships to get you around them. You will find that you have more energy during the day when what seem like major obstacles are quickly dealt with so you can be efficient with your day. Having an accountability partner can definitely help you in this process. That person might be a coach, mentor, associate, friend, or even a spouse. Just knowing you have to report back to someone other than your negotiable self is a sign that you are serious about executing your goals.

HEALTH

Take your wellness program seriously. If you don't have one at your company, create your own. More importantly, get one started at your company. Keeping yourself in the best possible condition to navigate at optimum capacity during the day will benefit you directly. Develop the great habit of following a workout regimen at least three days a week to keep your engine strong. When you decide to take charge of your health, you will replace bad habits with good ones, and the good ones will quickly become natural for you. You will feel empowered when you prove you are not a prisoner to your habits. It is a great joy to know that the free will we were given is a blessing we can exercise every day. Therefore, it is an easy choice to make great choices.

My business plan includes a belief in "healthy mind, healthy body." We all have tight schedules, deadlines, and agendas to manage. One essential activity you must time block on your agenda and execute to save your life is exercise. Exercising increases energy levels, helps you sleep better, and improves your focus. Don't get discouraged if you miss a few days, or even a few weeks of exercising. It happens! Just get started again and work back into your consistent momentum.

Having a fitness coach is one way people commit to a consistent schedule—and it provides that accountability partner I talked about earlier. If investing in a fitness coach will help you make a commitment to yourself, then spend the money. Make good use of your money by doing what your coach recommends both in terms of exercise and diet.

DIET

Maintaining immunity protects you from disease and bodily complications. Become a student of what foods contain the highest nutrient values. I am not a nutritionist, but I have observed that people who eat a balance of brightly colored vegetables with high levels of antioxidants tend to be healthier. These vegetables include greens, onions, bell peppers, kale, and tomatoes. Some of these yellow and orange vegetables contain nutrients called carotenoids, which benefit your vision, skin, bones, heart, and immune system.

Fruits like blueberries, strawberries, kiwi, blackberries, raspberries, and oranges contain antioxidants and can keep you from contracting diseases common to people who aren't watching their intake of unhealthy foods. Consuming the right nutrients will assist in weight control and higher energy levels.

Maybe you are attending too many prospecting/networking events and need to pay more attention to your health and diet. Too much of any good thing can turn out to be a bad thing. Getting enough sleep is also critical; sometimes, we just need to stop what we are doing and simply get some sleep. You recharge your car, smartphone, and computer, so make a point of recharging yourself to be your best. Make sleep a non-negotiable.

You owe yourself the benefit of knowing how to stay healthy. It is important to take care of your business' biggest asset—yourself—because it is what gets you to your different events and guards you from disease and toxins when you have to be at your best.

Another resource to be keenly aware of is slow-absorbing foods like beans, seeds, and nuts. The starches from these resources are disseminated through the body over a period of hours so the body can handle the inflow. By contrast, sugars and other carbohydrates can cause insulin spikes that aren't as easy for the body to handle and can quickly turn to fat.

A plant-based diet is best. Meats are great too in the right proportions. If you are consuming meats, use them more as accents to your meals than as your primary diet. Meats actually raise a hormone when consumed called IGF-1 (Insulin-like growth factor 1). Like insulin, IGF-1 is an anabolic hormone that actually binds to the insulin receptor that promotes more fat storage.

Believe it or not, eating more slowly and chewing your food more helps your body to maintain a good immunity practice. You will find yourself getting fuller more quickly when you allow your body to process your consumption while you are eating as opposed to gorging yourself so fast that your body is struggling to keep up and just sends the food to fat storage.

Make sure you reach out to a medical consultant for your particular best health plan. Get your blood work done and see whether you are deficient in some body vitamins or minerals that can be supplemented with some great products that are out there. I use omega-3, D3, or Vitamin D supplements. Some people can use more iron or magnesium; it just depends on your chemical make-up what may benefit you the most.

LAUGHTER

Laughter can be a big part of employee retention. When laughter is shared, it binds people together and increases happiness and intimacy. Humor and laughter also strengthen your immune system, boost your energy, diminish pain, and protect you from stress' damaging effects. Laughter is a priceless medicine that is fun, free, and anybody can do it. How simple is that?

I can't recall the last time I heard someone say, "I don't know why I would work for her; she is always in a good mood, humorous, and makes me laugh." I believe most people are drawn to a person who exudes joy and happiness.

Laughter triggers the release of endorphins, the body's natural feel-good chemicals. Endorphins promote an overall sense of wellbeing and can even temporarily relieve pain. Laughter protects the heart. Laughter improves the function of blood vessels and increases blood flow, which can help protect you against a heart attack and other cardiovascular problems. Laughter lowers stress hormones, relaxes your muscles, and enforces resilience.

Some of the social benefits of laughter are strengthened relationships, attracting others to us, encouraging teamwork, defusing conflict, enhancing group bonding, and promoting a sense of community.

COACHING AND MENTORS

Seek out those better than you. If you look around at whom you hang out with and you find you are the smartest one in the group, it is time to find a new group. If you become complacent or feel you have gotten off the journey because you have arrived, you are about to have a rude awakening. It is about the journey. We never get *there*. We do get to the next challenge that calls for our very best, but the good news is there will always be a space to improve in.

I am talking about mentors who do what you do really well. You might find them by researching who is the most successful at recruiting in your state, in the nation, or even internationally. Other people's experiences and scenarios will put you on the fast track to saving you time in your quest to be the "best" in your environment. Sometimes that comes through coaching.

Two prominent companies are leaders in the mortgage business: "Building Champions®" and "Buffini and Company™." Check into your industry to learn which coaching companies are the most highly recommended. Top performers in every department in your company are striving to advance and may be looking outside of your company for that kind of growth. Your people may see something in you that they aspire to be. If you have had coaching, you know it has improved your game. The structure I received in my business, life, and personal plans empowered me to achieve more in a measurable environment than I had experienced prior to coaching.

Coaching also allows you to pay it forward. You are called out to be the coach. Coach your people. Your people will appreciate the investment you make in them if you participate in sponsoring their fee for coaching. I have never completely paid for coaching because I want my people to feel some investment in the process, but I do think it is important to contribute to someone's growth.

John Yokoyama, the owner of Seattle's world famous Pike Place Fish Market, talks about "getting past your ego" in his book *When Fish Fly*. If you haven't seen the advertisements with his fishmongers throwing fish to clients and to each other, let me tell you it is truly fun to witness. John likes to create an environment where everyone is open to coaching. When one of his fishmongers sees a team member not fulfilling the company's established vision to be "world famous," he is naturally called upon to step in and empower that person.

John believes coaching works well when the coach creates a culture of empowerment. Effective coaches do not judge others but take responsibility for what they themselves are doing. They are suggesting and recommending, not ordering. They are inviting people to check alternative ways of thinking and being. They actually encourage other people to take charge of themselves. Coaching reflects a person's deeply held commitment to empower teammates into action.

Hopefully, by this point in the book, you are feeling inspired and you may have already unknowingly begun inspiring others around you. It doesn't hurt to pause here for a moment to look back at what you have overcome. How you have persevered and stayed the course in your career? You have made up your mind to be successful in recruiting, and you have made no excuses for some minor failures. You can feel good about some risk you have taken. Putting yourself in front of more prospects, engaging someone you feel might be out of your league, or taking action when typically you wouldn't have in an uncomfortable situation will help you continue to grow more. When you do find someone you feel may be out of your league, find a way to be around that person regardless. Make him or her coffee, secure game tickets, suggest a favorite salon (that you go to), or get the person an invitation to an event he or she really wants to attend.

Do what it takes to learn more about what you do or what someone two levels above you does. Perhaps you can ask that person to be your mentor; you may even be surprised to find that you have skills and abilities the other person can learn from. The two of you can then coach and mentor one another.

READ

Walt Disney once said, "We keep moving forward, opening new doors, and doing new things, because we're curious and curiosity keeps leading us down new paths."

One of the best ways to move forward and satisfy your curiosity is to read everything that makes you better at your craft. Then share what you've learned by reading—simply spread information in a friendly and helpful way. Did you read a book that someone in your network will enjoy? I am sure you already have an online bookstore you use, so *buy that person a book*.

Are you reading something that would help a friend with a project she is working on? Email it to her! Send it her way. Building your network is the same as building friends. Be interested in what others are doing and offer friendly suggestions when you can.

You have to be aware of the "soft stuff." Be authentic!

WORK SMARTER, NOT HARDER

No one can get you moving like you can get you moving. I know that not trying hard (truly giving it your best) is the issue that needs to be recognized. We can all fall out of the energy cycle we need to sustain the objective. A lot of times, lack of desire is a lesser issue, and not the main issue. Most people are trying hard and do want to improve. You are one of those people or you wouldn't be reading this book.

Identify exactly what your obstacles are as opposed to working harder to compensate for it. In other words, work smarter, not harder. Will and diligence always prevail, and we all need to have the self-control and discipline to see our objectives through.

Internal check. How successful have you been? After reading this book, will you say, "That advice was good. I should do some of those things." And then will you make excuses not to do them? Is there any reason why you won't take yourself seriously and execute? Are you already preparing your mind to make a change in your thinking about how you are going to accomplish what you know you need to do in this new recruiting environment? If you're already implementing before you get to the end of this book, that's great!

PREPARE AND BE DISCIPLINED

Identify your obstacles. Really analyze why you are hitting the wall! Freedom comes when obstacles aren't littering your path to the prize. You have solidified your culture and you are motivated, but you simply aren't following through. You begin to get that hopeless feeling and start to veer off course. A lot of times, veering off course results from a lack of discipline and preparation around your day. Discipline is defined by *Merriam-Webster's Dictionary* as, "training that corrects, molds, or perfects the mental faculties or moral character." Preparation is defined as "things that are done to make something ready or to become ready for something." With preparation comes confidence.

We all get overwhelmed when our capacity is being breached. We experience setbacks, fatigue, discouragement, and distractions.

If your solution is to try harder, it will only leave you feeling exhausted and hopeless. You need to rely on the disciplines and preparation you have established for yourself. You need to execute the well thought-out discipline you created when you weren't in the middle of what seemed like a storm. Then when you do experience storms, your discipline and plans to move forward will make your navigation easier.

Lean on your confidants; tell them your plans and bounce your ideas off them for additional confidence. Accountability is contagious. People actually want to know where the rudder is. Are we on a well-planned and executed course? If your purpose seems blurry, you may find that meeting more often as opposed to periodically will benefit you more. If you find you don't have enough structure around your disciplines, then establish consequences for not completing tasks. Some consequences you could try are: you have to put $10 in a jar when you don't execute a task, or you can't start the next book you want to read until you finish this one. Don't beat yourself up too badly, but do make the consequence significant enough that you will be sure to execute to the bar you have set for yourself. After all, this is supposed to be a hoot—not a guilt trip.

You can ignite that inspiration spark by intentionally putting in your life plan a quarterly commitment to experience something new. That new something can be as simple as listening to a different kind of music or as grandiose as skydiving. The key is to do something that stretches you and gives you something to look forward to that energizes creativity in your mindset.

AUTHENTICITY

One of the most valuable commodities you can possess as a leader is authenticity. Without authenticity, you are not considered a trusted leader.

In our process of seeking greatness, you may just lose the very thing that makes people trust you in the first place. The perception you give through how you behave, react, feel, and assess determines who will come to work with you. People will quickly align with you when you make your values system transparent. In all of your interactions with people, be true to yourself and don't waver to the world's whims.

In conversations with your prospects, if you come from a place of corporate speak, you will not be trusted. Driving on an initiative that appeals only to you is a disappointment to your prospect. Don't do that.

People will observe you being true to your values, your vision for the future, how you react to chaos, and how you approach problems. You are being watched by subordinates, so when a prospect makes a call to one of your subordinates to see what you are really like, how do you think your character will be relayed?

When you are consistent with your values system and transparent in your objectives, it attracts everyone. If people know they can rely on your consistent guiding hand and unflappable determination to succeed, they will follow and actually replicate your behavior. Even if people are not aligned with you, they need to know where they stand with you. Today, with so much social media interaction, people want to know who *you* are and what you stand for. As leaders, we have to make unpopular choices at times, but people will respect that a well thought-out decision will imminently be coming from you.

As a leader, you will gain long-term recognition from people, which will form a reputation for you before someone even meets you. As you meet people in the recruiting process, a lot of choices must be made by both you and the prospect. For you, maybe it's determining the potential, skill set, personality, initiative, and honesty of a particular applicant being considered. For the prospect, it may be ABC Company vs. XYZ Company, benefits here vs. benefits there, this location vs. that location.

Being authentic or genuine just means being your complete self—no more and no less. When you are completely honest and you speak from your heart, you will exude the kind of energy that people cannot help but connect with. In that moment, you are pure, expressive, and radiating your true self. When others see and recognize that side of you, they are really seeing a reflection of that part of themselves, which comes from a place of honest self-assessment. Being true to yourself and others means not being phony or having underlying agendas. Benefitting people in your network and getting help from them should be an exciting option for you daily. Recreate those moments after having interaction with a network member by remembering how energized you felt during and after that interaction. The more energy you feel, the more synergy you create for you and those around you. (We'll discuss synergy in more detail in Chapter 9.)

At times, you will find your team mired in self-doubt as a result of a dwindling pipeline of *good* prospects. It is up to you to refocus efforts and keep the enthusiasm alive for the big picture of building a world class team. When decisions are made from a place of authenticity by all parties, decisions come much more quickly and have focused alignment. People will gain confidence and trust through you when they know you have been authentic and you have shared some pain. That is a perfect time to set the example for authenticity. Here's how:

- **Recognize the pain.** Don't downplay it or desensitize it. Focus on being excited about the other person's status or objective by putting yourself in his or her shoes and imagining that your own career successes ride on your team's results. Your people will respect how genuine you are.

- **Show a little humility.** Don't be afraid to look human, and when you need help, ask for it. Nobody has all of the answers all the time. Your teammates will feel a point of satisfaction if they know you are human as well. "Get *you* out of the way of being authentic." When your team members get to help you solve a problem, they become more vested in the group effort.

- **Socializing with your group.** Socializing with your employees used to be taboo according to old school thinking; however, I can't encourage you enough to let people see who you are outside of the work environment. Practice being approachable. That not only holds true with your coworkers, but in your social interactions away from them. In any discussions with network contacts—whether phone calls, face-to-face discussions, or group settings—the priority should be providing help, insight, advice, and support for career problems, or even at times (when asked), personal problems.

- **Share what you have learned.** Share with your referring partners, coworkers, and contacts when you have learned something the hard way. Maybe it is a snag in your career growth, a particular problem unique to your particular industry, or an oops that you just experienced. The quasi think tank that engages brings authenticity around an initiative. Celebrate a win, or when you hear that others hit a snag or hit a win, make it a habit to share the experience so all may benefit. The more frequent the contacts, the more invested each of you will be in the others' success.

Everyone has real needs, both personally and professionally. With so many distractions with social media and the surface relationships that result from it, people are thirsty and crave real and meaningful relationships. Isn't it appropriate, then, to let people know you are there to offer assistance as a trusted source when needed? Don't you appreciate it when others do the same for you?

BECOME A GREAT STORYTELLER

Being a great storyteller so you can clearly define the picture of your culture, vision, and the future as it relates to your prospect is another excellent skill to possess. If you can offer up an antidote for a situation you know your applicant has experienced or an example of a problematic situation for your company where a solution was found, you will gain the trust of your audience.

I'm encouraging you to become a great storyteller by truly appreciating what you have to offer, understanding how it relates to what people need, and finding the most effective way to communicate a person's potential to succeed at your company. You have experiences no one else has had. Just carve out some time to sit down, rewind your life, and share some of your relevant stories. To grow, you need to put yourself in a constant state of challenge.

I am surprised by the number of leaders I speak to who still miss an unbelievable number of opportunities to share their company's accomplishments and true capabilities. In other words, they aren't good storytellers. Why? Because they don't know the whole process.

To be a great storyteller, you must first be a great listener. To find alignment in purpose and passion with another person, you need to be able to share the appropriate story at the appropriate time. Share a story that happened to you, a story that had an outcome similar to what your prospect is seeking, or a story of someone overcoming the odds as the result of a relationship with your company.

I have told the following personal story many times to illustrate how the slightest miscommunication can have disastrous effects:

I had passed enough of my flight training to be positioned to do my first solo flight. I was taxiing out to the runway as my flight instructor, Phil Casey (retired Navy pilot), was making his way up the tower to listen to my radio transmissions with the tower. As I approached the threshold, I remembered how my instructor had drilled into me not only to make my radio requests to the tower of my intent at the airport, but to make eye contact with the tower to make sure its personnel had their eyes on me.

I radioed, "Tower, this is 68 Uniform requesting permission to advance to the threshold." Tower responded, "68 Uniform, advance to the threshold and hold your position." I replied, "68 Uniform advancing and holding." Up to this point, my instructor was sharing with the air controller how well I was doing with my training. After what I felt was an exceptionally long time, I made another request to the tower: "68 Uniform requesting to advance to the runway for an immediate take-off with a right turn at the end of the runway." I had been trained to make sure the tower responded with full instructions for how to enter and exit the runway. For example, "Do an immediate take-off and exit left at the end of the runway." I made eye contact with the tower and made the request,

"68 Uniform requesting an immediate take-off exiting right at the end of the runway." The tower's response: "Okay."

I was looking at the tower, and the tower personnel were looking at me. "Okay" wasn't the full response I was looking for, but I thought, "He sees me; I made a full request; I'm going."

I throttled up and advanced to the runway. I immediately heard the tower personnel yelling, "68 Uniform, HOLD YOUR POSITION!" The next thing I heard was "78 Foxtrot, GO AROUND! GO AROUND!" as a twin engine plane went full throttle right over my head, quickly coming into view in my windshield. I had just pulled out in front of a plane about to land. The next transmission (in an irritated tone) I heard was, "68 Uniform, what are you doing down there?" I replied, "I made a full request of my intent to proceed down the runway and you responded with 'Okay'?"

The tower replied, "While you were transmitting to me, I was responding to 78 Foxtrot on his final. You heard the last part of my transmission to 78 Foxtrot."

I was in shock. I had been trying to impress my instructor with how well I was picking up this flying thing, but instead, I had probably put a couple of gray hairs on his head in seconds. I had almost caused a very bad accident on my first solo flight. I was relieved when I next heard, "68 Uniform, you may now do an immediate take-off with a right-hand turn at the end of the runway. Have a safe flight!"

Obviously, the importance of good communication cannot be underestimated. And I just impressed that importance upon you through the power of telling a story. Think how powerful acquiring the skill of telling good stories can actually be.

Have you ever felt the desire to grip a crowd in such a way that you could move it to action? Nothing grabs our attention, holds our attention, or moves us like a good story. And when a good story meets a great storyteller, great things can take place. If you are looking to become a dynamic communicator and an exceptional speaker, then you must learn the fine art of storytelling. Storytelling is an art, and it needs to be developed.

Storytelling is a cherished tradition and an entertaining, effective way to convey information about almost any subject. Walk into any classroom and you will find teachers educating their students with stories. Walk into a major corporation and you'll find high profile CEOs expressing thoughts, opinions, and facts to their employees with stories. Wherever you go, storytelling is a powerful means of communication.

Each of us has a desire, and perhaps even a need, to tell and to hear stories. By sharing stories and listening to those of others, we learn to understand one another at a much deeper level. By creating a common level of understanding, we come together as a community of individuals, appreciating both the differences and similarities we share.

So how do you go about becoming a great storyteller? How do you develop the fine art of using stories to make your speech more dynamic? Here are some steps to becoming an exceptional speaker and a great storyteller:

1. **Discover the #1 place for finding good stories…your own life!** That's right; you are the greatest resource for your own stories. While many public speakers, preachers, and teachers borrow stories from books, the Internet, and others, the best place to get your stories is your own life and experiences. Listen to the best public speakers and you will find they have one storytelling trait in common: the stories they tell are their own, not taken out of a book. There is nothing wrong with using stories from other places, but those resources just do not compare. Here's why: When we tell a personal story, we tell it with more energy and more passion than when we tell someone else's story. And passion is contagious! We are much more likely to inspire people to respond when we speak with great conviction and enthusiasm.

2. **Learn how to find the best stories from your life.** Carry with you a recorder or a notebook and pen. Anytime something moves you—makes you laugh, cry, think, become angry, etc.—write it down. And don't just write down a brief title; write in detail what happened. Over time, you will forget the details, so write down as much as you can as soon as you can. Then file it where you can find it the next time you need an illustration to drive home a specific point. Speaking of which…

3. **Make sure your story drives home your point!** I have actually seen a few public speakers (and more than a few preachers) tell stories just to tell them. They either do it simply to entertain or because they have failed to find a real illustration that actually makes the point. You never

want to use your story to drive your speech. Your story is just a tool for effective communication. If you are using stories to make your presentation more effective, it stands to reason that your stories should illustrate your point, not the other way around.

4. **Know your story inside and out!** The better you know your story, the more confidence you will have when you speak. This confidence is good for you, but it is very important for your audience, as well. Have you ever watched a speaker or singer who lacked confidence? As you sat in the audience, you couldn't wait for the performance to be over, not because you thought it was bad, but because you felt bad for the presenter. It made you nervous, and you weren't even the one on stage. If you are uncomfortable on the platform, your audience will be uncomfortable watching you. Please do not underestimate this point: Knowing your story inside and out is liberating and powerful. Be prepared. Be confident so you can own the stage.

5. **Tell your story with passion!** Another reason you want to know your story well is because it frees you up to tell your story with passion. When you do not have to worry about remembering all the important details of the story, you can focus your energy on your delivery. By expressing your love for something, you draw people to you and to what you are passionate about. You may be talking about something that somebody else cares about just as much as you do. Your passion about a particular topic can be inspiring to others who are seeking some inspiration.

A lot of people out there are looking for something they can be passionate about.

6. **Connect with your audience.** Connecting with your audience on an emotional level is huge. If you are able to connect with the crowd, you'll keep people interested and your story won't fall on deaf ears. This means understanding who the people in your audience are, what they desire, why they are there, and how to speak to them. Be sure to match how you speak with whom you are speaking to. Your tone, language, and attire should be different when you're talking to high school students versus a group of women over forty. Try to understand precisely what the audience goes through day-in and day-out so you can tell a story that connects with them.

7. **Use the story's emotion to compel your audience.** One reason so many successful public speakers use stories is because they have learned the great truth of emotion. Stories are so compelling because not only do they inform and entertain, but they bring about emotion; they inspire. Some stories make us laugh, some make us cry. Some stories make us think, some cause us to question. But all stories, if used right, can do the same thing— move us. A good story compels the audience to respond. Use the emotion of the story.

I want to share with you one other personal story I tell from time to time when I am trying to display humility, naivety, or perhaps a lack of preparation.

My wife, Taryn, and I were invited to a wedding when we were twenty-five years old and expecting our first son, Jason. The groom was Bob Brower, and he was marrying former President Richard M. Nixon's niece. We were excited to attend our friend's wedding, as well as to meet a former President of the United States. President Nixon was in the reception line at the wedding. I also had my camera and was shooting pictures of the wedding. As we proceeded through the line, I was asked by a Secret Service man whether he could speak with me for a minute. My wife looked at me like "What did you do now?" When I got back into the line with Taryn, I let her know the Secret Service had just wanted to check out my camera. I admit that incident rattled me a bit.

We did get to meet the new Mrs. Brower and the former President. In a bold moment, I asked whether President Nixon would be willing to have his picture taken with Taryn and our soon to be first son. He graciously complied. I snapped the picture and then asked for one more favor. My wife will never let me forget it. I asked, "President Nixon, will you bless our baby?"

Taryn looked at me and, in her calm tone, said, "Jeff, President Nixon is not a pastor!" I saw the Secret Service people chuckling, but the President graciously responded, "What is your soon-to-be son's name?" When I replied, "We haven't settled on a name for sure," President Nixon autographed a napkin and signed it, "To Baby X, Richard M. Nixon."

The clincher: The battery was dead in my camera. I still have the napkin, but no picture.

You can become an exceptional speaker and a dynamic communicator as an attractant. Whether it be in one-on-one situations or in a group setting, storytelling is a great skill to possess. Public speaking does not have to be something to fear or dread; it can be something you love to do. You simply need to develop the fine art of storytelling!

Fully own who you are and continually gain insight into what attracts the top talent. Becoming the "employer of choice" is easy to do if you are taking notes on what you learn here and making changes in how you are currently recruiting.

CHALLENGE

This week, focus on how you can take the stage by speaking at three events this year where your target group is in the audience. Take the time to research several associations or organizations that would benefit from your expertise. Find out where your peers may be presenting. Get comfortable with the speaker selection process for the venues where you would like to participate. Set the expectation at the beginning of your presentation and describe some of the takeaways that your audience will come away with. Knowing the benefit they are about to receive creates the excitement around what you are about to present.

Below, list the three events you plan to attend:

1. _____

2. _____

3. _____

Now think about the purpose of your presentation. List the top three takeaways your audience can expect to come away with.

1. _____

2. _____

3. _____

Remember, execute; then celebrate.

CHAPTER 4

NETWORKING

"If you don't do this, you won't get that."

— Author Unknown

What a privileged position you are in as a recruiter—you get to select and hire the people you will be working with. If you think about it, most people don't have that privilege. However, "To whom much is given, much is expected." Don't take your position for granted.

Being actively involved in an association that deals specifically with your industry is one of the most direct ways to find out who is the "Best" in your industry. Your exposure in the association also attracts attention to those within the association who might be considering a career change. Movers and shakers want to be kindred to those who are movers and shakers. At any business event you attend—be it a seminar, association meeting, or philanthropic event—make a point of sitting with people you don't know. It is easy and comfortable to sit with people you know, but that is definitely not the way to meet people you don't know or would like to know. Sitting at a venue and conversing with someone during breaks or before and after the presentation can result in you naturally falling into an opportunity because both of you are exploring a new acquaintance who may be looking for a change or a new challenge.

By placing yourself around people who are making things happen, you move further away from your routine of typical acquaintances and expand your environment to one of unforeseen relationships that continue to multiply. I see a lot of recruiters who sink into their own small comfortable environment. If you continue to do that, you will always get the same results. You are looking for more, aren't you? We need others to stimulate our creativity, inspiration, energy, and forward progress.

At times, networking requires you to be audacious. At times, you will feel like you are batting way out of your league and someone may be way beyond your reach in the world of networking. Do your homework. *Everyone* is approachable if you have the right approach. What might be a connecting point between you? Did you go to the same college? Have you worked with the same company? Do you like the same sports team?

Personal relationships are still the very best way to put yourself and your company in front of the people you want to be in front of.

In his book *Love is the Killer App,* Tim Sanders teaches you how to become the "lovecat." Tim defines the lovecat as a "business person who is known for sharing and being a promoter of business growth." It is a mindset that I try to apply daily in my pursuit of great relationships. I would suggest picking up this fabulous read and devouring it. One of my favorite comments that Tim makes is "Nice guys don't finish last. THEY RULE!"

Being sincere in your efforts to bring benefit to your contact is an obvious attractant. You can commit a foul in the recruiting game when you expect something in return for your efforts. Just because you reached out and made contact with someone does not put that person in your debt. Consider yourself how uncomfortable you feel when someone is requiring you to pay him back. Instead of approaching networking with the goal of gaining future markers due, try reaching out in humility and with curiosity.

Being genuinely curious and learning from someone else who might have something to teach you is time well invested. If you are listening intently to the person in front of you and really capturing the obstacles she is dealing with, it gives you the perfect opportunity to consider some solutions that might help her. Listening closely will give you the opportunity to follow up later by sending her a favorite book she mentioned, flowers you know she likes, tickets to that game she mentioned, or a gift card to a new restaurant she wants to try.

In most cases, your excitement toward someone else's issue will be viewed as charming and authentic and be accepted.

GENEROSITY

One of the hardest things to accomplish when someone is reasonably happy with a current employer is to get him or her excited about the opportunity you have to offer. Quite frankly, no one is going to be that excited about your opportunity if he or she does not feel compelled to move. Your best networks should contain the best and the brightest in your industry. The business world is very competitive, and the general consensus is that if you want to be the best, you should not help others to be great. But that is old school.

Until you understand that no one gets to the top on his own, true success will continue to elude you. You can't be the best without others' help or without recognizing them for that help in achieving the success you enjoy. The truth is that if you don't understand the reason why you are experiencing success, you have missed the point of what got you there. Recruiting is a mutual endeavor that includes the people you are seeking out, the people who can assist you in networking to those people, the staff that assists in a smooth onboarding, and the people who will speak well of you when prospects are doing their homework on you.

Investing unselfish time and energy into others should become instinctive for you. The unexpected dividends you receive always seem to come at just the right time. Be generous with your knowledge, contacts, skills, and expertise. Never keep score!

The perpetuation of your sphere of contacts will continue to grow because people see you as being generous and want to help you. Something as simple as being generous with your smile can help.

SMILE

Just think about how you feel when someone flashes you a genuine smile? How does it feel when you are out of your normal travel area, you are alone, and you feel awkward in a particular place? Then, suddenly, someone smiles at you! Admit it; it's contagious. A smile can immediately shift your state to a positive one. A simple smile can lift the spirits of the person you are engaging or maybe even those of a passing stranger.

A smile is just short of the one thing we all desire as humans—human touch from a loved one. A lot of information is conveyed in a smile—perhaps someone has made you happy, amused you, or is proud of himself or you. A smile can be a simple acknowledgment that someone is important enough for you to smile at her. Smile genuinely.

Just don't expect anything in return, or you have totally missed the point of sharing and making those around you better.

NETWORK WITH INTENT

By networking with intent, I mean have a plan. When attending a networking event, decide early on what you want to come away with. Try going into an event with simple objectives, such as meeting three people you have never met before, or asking someone you know at the event to introduce you to someone you need to know.

As you become more confident at these events (through practice), you will be setting bigger goals for yourself, and you will begin to look forward to networking events. You will naturally start stepping up from meeting one or two people to groups of people to full company opportunities.

If you can gain access to an attendee list prior to the event, you will have an advantage because you will know who will be there and can plan in advance how to strike up a conversation with someone you want to develop a quick relationship with.

Having intent will keep you more focused and productive within the short time frames typical at networking events. When you show up to these events prepared and informed, you will find yourself noticeably more comfortable because you have empowered yourself to prevail.

A thin line exists here that you need to be wary not to cross. If you are pursuing *your* agenda a little too hard on your first foray into a networking group, people will find that offensive and feel like they are being sold on something. I don't like that. You don't like that. Don't do it!

You're trying to develop a relationship with someone, which means you should be thinking about that person, not you. It's your mission to understand the people in your network, where they are coming from, and what's important to them. Success will be fleeting if it is about you.

Keep in mind that you are there to develop relationships, not force your agenda. If you look or act desperate, people will find that annoying. Instead, share information and engage people in topics you know are important to them. As you provide benefit to your newfound relationships, people will want to know more about you and your company. Make it easy on yourself here.

I know I have achieved the desired result when someone asks me for my business card or offers me her vCard so we can get back to each other. I very seldom offer my contact information first. I don't indiscriminately nor freely shotgun my cards or emails for that matter to everyone I meet. You don't need to have the largest sphere of influence; you just have to have the right people within that sphere. Find the people who are relevant to you and your company. We will cover prospecting in the next chapter. As your relationship blossoms with your contact, you can decide whether alignment is occurring. It is better to have ten people willing to help you than 200 who just know your name.

Most of you have heard many times that one of the sweetest things a person can hear is his or her own name. Including people's names in conversation a time or two is a must. It will also help you re-member their names. Along the same lines of social courtesy, when receiving someone's business card, take the time to acknowledge his information and comment on it before putting it in a place where you won't lose it. That one act alone shows that person that you are sincere in getting back to him.

Whether you are a male or female executive, shake hands like a burly logger every time, and look your newfound friend straight in the eye. A firm handshake tells tons about your fortitude and your will-ingness to engage someone. A weak handshake is just that. Weak!

More times than not, networking events seem to include alcohol. In a business situation, it is of the utmost importance to project and maintain a professional persona. Having a drink or drinks will put you at risk of compromising a relationship that you really wanted to open up. With your inhibitions not in check, saying the wrong thing or maybe saying too much can put you into a regret posture. I don't want that for you.

Having a non-alcoholic drink in a business situation may actually make you aware of some conversations going on around you where people may very well be saying a little more than they should. You can use that to your advantage by knowing whom you don't want to do business with, but at the same time, avoid gossiping about others because it will only reflect badly on you in the long run.

Remember also, networking is the place to initiate and build relationships. It is not the place to close the deal. Networking is the venue to open new relationships, follow up on previous commitments, introduce parties who need to know each other, and possibly make an appointment to close the deal. Trying to close a deal at a networking event can put someone in an awkward position in front of peers. It is like trying to get a kiss on the first date. Awkward!

Extend your networking efforts with your current employees by offering incentives to help draw people to your company. Energized employees are a recruiter's best advocates. When prospective employees hear great things about your company from current employees, they are not as suspect that the information they are receiving is a little too positive.

Incent your current employees to make it rain. Offer them a signing bonus: $1,000 for the first ninety days and another $500 when the new hire completes six months of employment. Then current employees are vested in the success of their referral to the company. You could also base a percentage of the new hire's first six months of commission as a bonus to the referring employees paid once each quarter for the first year.

Golfing, tennis, wine tasting, boating, orienteering, philanthropy, and volunteering are all great ways to network. Be creative and meld your passions with your activities. Just be active and engaged. Have fun with it. The more you are out there, the more people will identify with you and what your company is about. Achievers and active people are drawn to each other.

Be creative and accommodating in your events. I have done open houses (1st, 2nd, 3rd Grand Openings at the same location), invited the right people into our company for wine tastings with Billy O wines, sponsored meet the mayor events, introduced prospects to the company president and owners, shown them locations for prospective branches, and awarded people for simply showing up with gift certificates for dinners to favored restaurants, movie passes, highly coveted wines, and company branded marketing items.

Conduct sales skills training as a regular course of business and invite your prospects to those events so they can see how proactive your culture is toward cutting edge sales skills.

Head up your state's mortgage industry Legislative Day. Not only will it get your company recognized as an industry leader on initiatives vital to the industry's efficiency, but it will allow you to associate with the kinds of people you want to play ball with at your company.

Get out of your industry! I mean implant yourself into other industries to expose your company to other possible recruits. Connect with people on a variety of levels from a wide range of industries and locations. By expanding your network outside of the usual areas, you will be more valuable to people in your immediate industry. The people you work with have passions and hobbies that they like to do in their free time, right? With a broad network, you can be the person who connects people across industries and kindred likes.

Capitalize on the possibilities by reaching out to a few key contacts in an unfamiliar industry and invite them to meet for coffee. Explain to the contacts that you admire their positions/expertise within their industries and are interested in learning more about how you can overlap their successes into your particular industry. You can also share some beneficial information with them that you recognize has worked in your industry and might enhance theirs.

In the last two years, I have started attending staged networking events attended by people from all types of industries, including healthcare, real estate, consulting, publishing, music, human resources, insurance, public speaking, investing, high tech, architecture, and on and on.

Network After Work™—Networking Events for Professionals is a national business and social networking event company that launched in June 2009. It currently hosts events in nineteen cities across the country. Events are created for professionals who want to expand their networks and create new business opportunities. They range in size from 150-600 professionals, and they take place in each city's top nightlife destinations. The events provide a relaxed atmosphere for professionals to market themselves and or/ their companies with some of each city's top business professionals. Everyone is there to network so there is no pretense about subtly working into the conversation what you do or what company you work for. Just get out there. Begin conversations by saying things like, "How can I help you?" "I have a client who is looking for an insurance guy right now." "My builder is looking for a new architect." Upon entering the event, each guest receives a color-coded nametag by industry that allows for easy navigation and cutting to the chase of what industry he or she is involved in. Complimentary cocktails and appetizers are provided for the first hour. Visit the company at http://networkafterwork.com

You can choose from a plethora of similar nationwide networking groups: Meetups, Atlanta event.com, Vistage, Omaha Roundtable, Topeka Networking Council, BNI Central Phoenix, and Real Estate 360, to name a few. Just pick one!

I found a great attractant to wear to these events called the Flash Badge (theflashbadge.com). It's a nametag that lights up with interchangeable screens and really can draw attention to you. Slap a Flash Badge on instead of a nametag and see the magic take effect. I have had people two deep standing in front of me trying to find out where I got the "bugs to light" badge. Curiosity will get the best of them. For some events, it might be a little on the obnoxious side to wear, but there is no shame in drawing a little attention your way. When in a room full of people who don't know each other, it is a little awkward just to drum up a conversation with a stranger, so I have found this to be a great icebreaker.

Speaking of icebreakers, it never hurts to have some icebreaker questions prepared that you can ask people. For example, "What is the most fun thing you get to do in your present position?" This question gets around just asking, "What do you do?" It's one of my favorite questions because it's really two questions in one. Another great question that provides a similar result is "What brings you joy in your present position?"

Ask "Who can I introduce you to?" once you've gained some insight into what interests the person you're conversing with. This question gives you the opportunity to show the person you care and bring value as an addition to his or her network. It boils down to the old adage "People don't care what you know until they know how much you care." As you listen to the types of people the person wants to meet, you might be able to introduce him or her to someone at the event, or maybe at a later date, you can make a referral.

Please remember to stay on topic during your engagement with your new contact. Listen attentively and don't be thinking of the next thing you are going to say. If you listen most of the time and speak less of the time, far better results will come your way.

EXPOSURE: GOOD & BAD

Projecting your company's brand and culture into your networking events can create great exposure. As you receive information, look for opportunities for great exposure; then implement the skill sets you are learning for disciplined follow-up, implementation, and execution. You become more sought out, your friends become more sought out, and everyone benefits just from knowing each other.

What are you currently doing to keep yourself focused on achieving the kind of recruiting success you desire? For example, are you educating yourself, attending the right networking opportunities, dedicating yourself to your daily disciplines, and investing in others?

In the same way, bad exposure is something to be acutely aware of. Who are you hanging out with? You are the average of the five people you spend the most time with, and others will know you by the company you keep. So with whom are you spending your time? Are they well-connected? Are you in the same step with the achievers you seek to hang out with and who seek to hang out with you?

Really think about whom you spend the most time with. Do those people possess the same moral compass, values, and aspirations you do or that you are working on achieving? Are you all reading the same books, referring the same professionals, continuing to gain credibility both socially and professionally, attending the same educational opportunities, and sharing ideas with each other?

BUSINESS DEVELOPMENT DEPARTMENTS AND COMPANIES

Recently, business development departments have been having success with capturing talent. However, a business development department is a luxury for most managers, especially at smaller companies. However, if your company has a business development team and it's focused on the same principles and practices outlined in this book, you, as a manager, can have a very fortified and effective recruiting machine to work well with.

Weekly and, at times, daily reviews with your business development people (depending on how full the prospect bucket is) are a best practice. A prospect's mindset can be very anxious as he or she probes and questions what the lay of the land looks like at your company. If a prospect experiences a set of responses from you that are different from the responses he may get from your business development group, then that creates questions regarding whether your company is well-organized and everyone is on the same page. Those weekly and sometimes daily huddles, even if only for five minutes, can diminish most anxiety you may be unknowingly creating for the great hire you are pursuing.

When emailing a potential recruit, I have learned to "BCC" my business development team so any communication we have is across the board and everyone is on the same page with the process.

If you cannot yet employ a business development team, the good habits you are developing through applying the techniques in this book will leave you better prepared to hire the right people in business development when that time comes. Training your business development people with proven practices will give them confidence to promote your company's synergy and culture with excitement and pride.

For a company that can't afford an in-house business development team, some great private business development companies are out there that you can call on. Some companies work on a retained search basis while others charge a monthly fee with a discount on the recruiting fee. I have found most of these companies to be somewhat flexible based on the type of position you are looking to fill.

When interviewing a business development team, one of the key questions you will want to ask is, "How large is your database of prospects, and to what extent do you use it?" The discipline of cold calling on prospects is a special skill that some people just don't have the patience for. However, a good private business development company will have its personnel well-scripted on the cold call that represents your company so it can vet out the best prospects to present for your consideration.

After meeting with the business development company to discuss your vision, mission, and core values, you can let it bring the prospects to you.

Another advantage is a private business development company can host recruiting workshops. It is pretty tough for a midsize company to spend time and resources to keep up on all the nuances of the competition's evolving models. If you are considering moving into a particular market area, a business development company may have experience in that particular market area and be able to assist in defining whether your particular culture and business model would have a high rate of success in a particular market where it is already working. Typically, such companies have evaluated many different organizations, models, platforms, cultures, and everything else imaginable so you don't have to.

After you have selected a candidate whom you feel will thrive in your culture, your business development company can follow up for you. It can take care of presenting the offer, engaging the transition plan, and guaranteeing the placement by staying engaged with the candidate for the first sixty days of his or her employment.

INTRODUCTIONS

Make introductions often and with the right people. Always ask people for permission to introduce them to others. Never just assume that your new contact wants to be connected to someone you feel he or she could benefit from knowing. Remember, it is not about you; it is, however, about the other person. Put people in a position of power and they will like you. Make them feel like they were forced to make an acquaintance and you have hurt the relationship you had with them.

Connecting like-minded people is a powerful way to enhance your network. It is actually quite easy to do and becomes very natural with practice. Do you know two people who enjoy racing, hiking, reading the same type of books, collecting similar items, rooting for the same sports team, or who work in the same industry? You get the point. Don't make it hard; just introduce the two of them by sharing their common interest. They can decide whether they want to pursue the relationship further.

BEING RESILIENT

We all have experienced enough NO's or felt the rejection of our sincerest efforts not being appreciated. Being resilient when you don't feel like it is a learned skill. Some call it perseverance; some call it persistence. When you learn to be resilient, you will outperform all of your competitors. The thing I love most is when one of my competitors makes a statement like "This recruiting thing is so hard." Gotcha!

How can you become more resilient and bounce back from a minor setback? By the way, all setbacks are minor. Realize that the recruiting we do is one of the purest forms of sales out there. Its joy lies in selling futures and opportunities for people who may not have been introduced to those opportunities if it hadn't been for a recruiter.

So many variables come into play as we recruit; we have to deal with economic changes, someone deciding to back out at the last minute, or having a great prospect sign on with another company. Some things are just out of our control. Winners in this game keep their emotions in check and bounce back. At some point, we have all questioned our ability to perform in this career of recruiting. If you haven't, you just haven't been at it that long.

So how do you develop a mindset to remain unflappable? Here are the three tools you can use to help manage your emotions and win the day:

- **Perspective:** See the long range goal of creating, building, and expanding your environment. Always keep your eye on the bigger picture. Fall back into where you find your strength. That may be your faith, your family, or your passions outside of the work environment, or even spending time away on vacation. Live there and not in the moment that is currently interfering with the big picture. Tell yourself, "What just happened today, in the bigger scheme of things, is irrelevant to my ultimate success."

- **Compare:** What just happened today? How does that compare with other things in your past that you have faced and prevailed over? Getting a grip right here will immediately put you back into a state of performance. How bad is what just happened in comparison to what just happened to company XYZ, or how bad is it compared to your friend who just lost his wife to cancer? There is always a situation out there you can reflect on that makes your present situation seem pretty minuscule. We never want to revel in the place of someone else's pain, but we do want to be aware that no matter how bad our current situation may seem, someone out there always has it worse.

- **Be detached from the outcome:** External circumstances over which you have no control can derail the particular expectation you set. When that happens, can you be disappointed? Sure! Can you let it ruin you? No!

When you are leading a great company and your efforts are recognized as part of the reason why that particular company is enjoying its success, you will be getting recruited by other companies. If you weren't great at what you are doing, you wouldn't be getting those calls. Don't be above going on an interview yourself. Go on an interview with a company that interests you. Some of the best opportunities present themselves when you aren't even considering making a change.

I often share the following story with people I'm recruiting whom I'm finding it difficult to meet face to face. I was playing golf with a future mortgage company partner at a Young Life golf tournament. At the time, I was happy as an employee with Golf Savings Bank, so I didn't even know about an opportunity to become a principal in a mortgage company I had never even heard of before that golf game. After a casual conversation with another player in the tournament, however, I learned about what the company was trying to do and how I might fit into the equation. Long story short, I become a principal of Homestead Mortgage.

When I'm having a hard time meeting with some of these prospects, the line I sometimes use is "I have come across some of the greatest opportunities in my career when I wasn't even looking." If you don't take the time periodically to poke your head out of your regular routine and explore options, you might be missing the dream gig you have always wanted. If nothing else, you can see how others do what you do, and you might pick up some tips on how to hone your skill set.

FEAR

I saved this topic for the end of this chapter so I didn't scare you off early and reinforce some people's sweaty palm, anxious, unsure attitudes toward networking. Fear can paralyze and make you ineffective so it needs to be put away. Take a proactive stance against fear. Talk about it with people—even the people you are engaging with at the next or maybe your first networking event. You will find many people want to help you. In my experience, the more you connect, the more second nature networking will become for you.

Throughout this book, I touch on preparation. With preparation comes confidence—confidence in knowing who are the people in the room, the topic of the event you are attending, and the initiatives at the event. How can you benefit the people attending the event?

You may be anxious about meeting someone at a networking event with whom you have a past history that didn't go so well. Role play with someone you know and trust who will walk you through a scenario of how that conversation might go. Then you can experience the fear and anxiety you might encounter and assess your options for responses. Having already experienced the event will give you confidence to deal with the fear. You can do it!

In the same way, knowing that someone at an event can make or break a major initiative you are pursuing can put a lot of pressure on you to have an excellent first encounter with that person. My best and most calming affirmation prior to that type of encounter is to tell myself, "This person puts his or her pants on every day just like I do. This person probably has kids, bills, and a car in the repair shop and will be shopping for groceries at the end of the day just like I do." Some people have nerves of steel and at times may display a sense of overconfidence. I can assure you that having a little fear is a great filter to keep you from appearing arrogant or self-indulged, neither of which are characteristics of an attractant.

The takeaway I want for you here is to realize that once you arrest the fear we all have—some minor, some major—you have just cleared another obstacle on your path to becoming an excellent recruiter.

CHALLENGE

List three different networking venues you are not currently attending that you will commit to attending in the next ninety days to stretch you out of your comfort zone.

1. _____

2. _____

3. _____

CHAPTER 5

PROSPECTING

"Be vewy quiet. We're hunting wabbits!"

— Elmer Fudd

Passive candidates have been my best hires. They are already employed and not actively job hunting. They are most likely to be your dream hires, but you will never attract them without letting them know how much you want them.

Phil Johnson, founder of Millstone Coffee and CEO/Chairman of Cascade Coffee, agrees that passive hires have been his best hires. Primarily through talking with his customers and suppliers, he has found out who is good at what they do and has hired the key person for each market area where he has wanted to increase his presence.

Passive hires are the easiest people to show your company to. They realize you are not selling them anything; you are, however, offering opportunities. Who isn't interested in an opportunity to increase his monetary gain or improve his life over what he is currently experiencing? This has got to be one of the easiest sales jobs in the world.

If you are making it a point to prospect for diversity, you will be enriching your work environment with different cultures, backgrounds, educations, faiths, and ethnic origins. You are also making your company a fun place to work. Embrace diversity and you will make your company much more attractive to others. No one is ever too old, too young, or too inexperienced to fit into your company's vision.

We tend to seek out and hire people just like us. This tendency should be avoided. It can really cramp your ability to grow as a person and as a company. Enhancing diversity gives you and everyone in your company the opportunity for new perspectives. Try to come from a more global perspective in your future hires. Everyone in an organization will benefit when more contrarian views are presented.

To be effective in presenting to your prospective talent, you do need to do your homework to find out what your competition is offering. You may have as good or better a widget, but you won't know that unless you take time to study your competition. Find out about the competition's pay structure from its former employees who may now be working with you. Following are some suggestions from the mortgage business. How can you apply some of these to your industry?

- Go out to builders' sites to see what programs are being offered.

- Grab flyers from realtors' listing boxes to see what type of programs the competition is offering. How good is the quality of their marketing?

- Lean into vendors for information on operating systems for both origination and client retention systems. What type of benefits are being offered? Your company may be using the same benefits management company.

- Ask the benefits representative what is being offered by your competition. Find out what the competition is offering for incentives.

If you are talking to the "best" people out there, chances are your competition is talking to those same people. Your prospects are comparing and analyzing and may share with you what they are finding out about your competition. Listen to them also when they give you feedback about "why" they are speaking to you in the first place during the interview or on your initial conversation. Their reasons might be as simple as "You do a better job in your marketing department," "I like your location better," or "I love your sales manager."

Keep in mind that the pay or benefits may not be the only reasons why someone wants to explore working with your company, although you do need to be competitive.

As you attend industry improvement seminars, remember that the other people attending are interested in improving themselves in their careers. Attend these events to look for prospects as well as improve yourself. Who knows? You might learn something new at one of these events.

TIME BLOCKING

Time blocking is critical to dedicating the time you need to invest in your recruiting effort.

Time block well by having purpose when you are making your prospecting calls. If your purpose is to obtain an interview, take the relationship to the next level. The people I know who time block well are busy and productive. Know your skills, know your limits, and delegate the rest. Time blocking is not trying to get everything done; it is getting the right things done.

I make a habit of answering my emails at 8:30 a.m., 11:30 a.m., and 3:30 p.m. You might even turn off your email alert balloons so as not to be distracted from your schedule for the day. If you are entering into your calendar daily time blocks for identifying whom you want to be making calls to and doing the follow up required for previous calls, then apps like SaneBox™ can assist you in managing your email traffic. If you were to do a time study on it, you would probably find that email is an area where you are spending too much time.

GetResponse™ analyzed more than 21 million emails sent the first quarter of 2012. Among the findings:

- 23.63 percent of all emails are opened within the first hour of the workday; that number drops off precipitously as the hours tick by.
- Most emails are sent from 6 a.m. to noon.
- The hours that see the most opens are 8 to 9 a.m., and 3 p.m. to 4 p.m.

Furthermore, "The best time to send emails is when professionals are reviewing their inboxes," and "For maximum open and click rates, choose morning and early afternoon."

Another great habit to get into is changing your phone greeting every morning. You are showing people you are building new relationships and that you are relationship-oriented. People don't want to hear the same old tired greeting of "You have reached Joey Boring. At the sound of the beep, please leave your name and number."

You might try "Hello, this is Ms. Approachable on Monday the 10th. I have an appointment this morning from 9:00 to 10:30, and another this afternoon from 2:30 to 3:00. Other than that, I will be available and in the office to assist you. Thank you for your call. I look forward to speaking with you."

You could even try: "Hello. This is Warm & Fuzzy. It's Monday the 15th, and I will be at our XYZ company charity golf tournament from 8:00 a.m. until 1:00 p.m. If in the meantime you need immediate attention, you can press 5817 to be forwarded to my team member Mr. Fix-It, and he will be happy to take care of you. I will be checking voice mails and look forward to speaking with you soon."

Show that you care that the caller didn't catch you live. Set the expectation for when he or she can expect to receive a callback from you. Subtly announce what is on the schedule with you and your company for the day. You are exhibiting that you are checking your voicemail throughout the day. People know they will be attended to. That first impression speaks a lot even in something as simple as your phone greeting.

INTRODUCTIONS AND COLD CALLING

I have found that cold calling is basically ineffective and gives the impression that you are desperate. Yes, there are times when you *have* to get some kind of a crack into a potential prospect for your company. If you find yourself in a place where you have no resources available through your existing network to reach out to someone, you may have to make the dreaded cold call. When you find yourself in that place, *always* start by offering praise or bringing benefit. It is best *not* to start with asking for help.

In some situations, you need to ask for something, but you don't have any reference place to start from. Most situations don't fall under this category, but if you must ask for something, then ask for permission before you make a request. I'll give you a personal example here.

I was trying to work an employee benefit program into a healthcare company where I didn't know the HR person. A contact of mine, Steve, gave me her name. I began the conversation by asking the HR person for permission to continue: "I've implemented this employee benefit program with another technology special interest group before and they loved it; would you like to know more?" She was interested, and we ended up being added to the company's in-tranet as its company-wide endorsed employee resource for lending, retailer discounts, and referring partners in the real estate industry.

An additional benefit of this strategy is that you are getting the other party to say, "Yes" to you. A general rule in most sales environments is that if you can get someone to say "Yes" three times, then the odds of your request being accepted by that person drastically increase. You don't need to ask permission for everything, but if you're opening a conversation where you will need to make a request, then this technique works.

Online introductions are more prevalent these days, and they can be effective. Here are some suggestions that have worked for me. You can coach your referring partners with what works best, and they can, in turn, use this method to enhance their prospecting as well.

Have your referral source send the email introduction to your prospect and CC you on the email. Make sure you ask him to do so and don't just assume he will. Respond in a time frame relevant to the prospect and urgency of the referral and include the referrer's name in the subject title. That first response is a key moment to take full advantage of the referral. Make sure to CC your referrer so he or she knows you are following up on a prized referral.

Keep your response to the prospect short and engaging. Some of my follow-ups have looked like this: "Mike asked me to reach out to you knowing that some of the options we were offering in lead generation might benefit you and your team in some of the areas where you are trying to make headway. Is there a good day and time this week when I could contact you to discuss what Mike thought we would find mutually beneficial?" or "Gary thought we could be more effective by combining resources. I would like to discuss that with you at a good day and time this week that would work for you."

Remember, you have not earned the right to ask for the person's business or close an employment opportunity at this point; you are merely establishing a comfortable environment within which the two of you or a group can meet.

A great practice that brings the "Wow effect" to your process is to include the spouse or significant other into the fold. It may initially appear a little forward to ask an applicant for his or her home address, but I always explain that we would like to acknowledge and thank the prospect's significant other for the time he or she allowed us to share with his or her loved one. I only do this with someone I have done my homework on and know is an ideal candidate for our company.

It is imperative that the "Wow effect" be implemented the day of the interview before the interviewee returns home that evening or, at the very latest, the next day. Open an account with your local florist, chocolate confectioners, gift boutique, local spa, party store, online bookstore, fragrance wholesaler, home enhancement store, or favorite restaurant. Be creative and use those companies to enhance the experience that people evaluating your company will appreciate.

With one prospect, I made sure a fruit basket shaped like a house would reach his house and spouse before he did. I attached a card that said, "Thank you so much for allowing us time today with your treasured husband. I personally want to extend an invitation to you to come by our office to receive a red carpet tour and meet some of the people your husband would be working with."

Later that evening, he called to tell me, "You are sure making it hard for me to have a reasonable conversation comparing other companies when nobody else is doing what you have done." He added, "My wife says your company is the one I should be working for." He accepted the position on that phone call and asked to get the paperwork started.

His wife did not come in to tour the office, but she did like the open invitation and that she was being empowered to be part of a life-changing decision.

Since the recent recession, budgets are tighter, so golf weekends, cruises, and huge signing bonuses are not as prevalent. However, nothing is wrong with offering bonuses based on historical performance by your prospective employee. In the mortgage business, paying an extra $1,000 per transaction to the loan officer when the buyer closes is a great incentive. Typically, this type of bonus is for the first sixty or ninety days of employment. As the producer closes business, you have the funds to pay him or her, and true producers will be challenged knowing they are getting a great incentive to do what they have historically done for business and maybe even try to outperform themselves. Then everybody wins!

In these cases, I have found satisfaction in knowing that if an originator comes in and goes dead leg on you, your company is not out of a signing bonus that probably shouldn't have been paid out to begin with.

Realtors, referring partners, and business associates are a great way to access a passive referral. Ask your referring partners "Other than me, who are you seeing approach you regularly?" You can ask whom, other than yourself or your company, the person has worked with who is really great competition in terms of what you offer in a business relationship. Then initiate some of the techniques you are learning here.

In the old days, I would, from time to time, ask my associates whom I did business with at escrow and title companies, "Who is pushing a lot of volume through your company and doing a clean job of it, and would you be comfortable introducing that person to me?"

I have pulled back on asking that question out of respect for the position I have put an escrow or title representative in because in the past I have been offered names of people who were sounding off their frustrations with their present employers. If the employer had got wind of the referral I had received, it likely would have ended in the loss of that company's referral business to my friend or associate, and perhaps even that person losing his job because I put pressure on him. Then nobody wins!

In respect to your well-established relationships, I've noticed that what goes around comes around. My retention of employees has been better when I'm not putting pressure on my escrow and title relationships. After all, those same associates might have been taking advantage of me when I had an employee experiencing a temporary meltdown.

Your reputation for ethics and integrity precede you in this fickle business of recruiting, and the smallest of errors can ruin you and your reputation.

I have heard stories of people who committed to working for a particular company after being oversold on the benefits, marketing, or pay splits they would receive, only to find none of that was true once they were hired. That situation not only hurts the recruiter's credibility, but it pretty much puts an end to your further success in prospecting within your industry once word gets out of what happened.

Conveying to someone you hardly know in a very short time frame that you are a person of integrity is not an easy task. We all have a neurotransmitter in our brains called dopamine. When it is activated by something good, such as the feeling of relief that your company's platform will bring to someone's daily regimen, it is a good thing. On the other hand, if something negative is received during a conversation that gives someone anxiety, such as you not being consistent with the information you are presenting, it can have a very negative effect toward what someone is assessing about you and your company.

The amygdala portion of our brains (an almond-shaped structure nestled in both the left and right temporal lobes) generates the fight or flee response. This is where dopamine has a large effect in processing positive emotions. However, it is better known for its role in processing fearful and anxious emotional states associated with potential threats to survival. Some refer to this as the bio reaction in a response to a situation that triggers a reaction from you.

As discussed earlier, in recruiting, we are trying to attract the people who believe what we believe. By that, I mean the people who believe as you do in the culture you have built. I want to get a little biological with you right now.

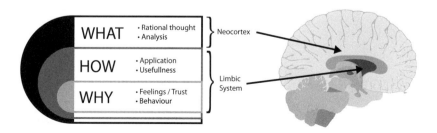

The human brain has three main parts: the cerebral cortex or neocortex and the two limbic portions. The cerebral cortex relates to the *what* around how our brain works. It is the rational part of the brain and where analytical thought originates. It is also where our language resides. The limbic part is in the brain's middle and relates to the *why* part of how we think. This part of the brain is responsible for our feelings, trust, loyalty, all human behavior, and all decision making. There is no language capacity, however, in this part of the brain. This area doesn't just drive behavior; it allows people to understand feature benefits, facts, and figures.

When we communicate externally, that communication is being received by the neocortex region of the brain. When we communicate internally, it's to the limbic brain, which controls behavior. The limbic brain is where you make decisions that you may refer to as your sixth sense or intuitive sense, allowing you to feel that an opportunity feels right or there is something about it that just doesn't feel right.

I mention all this information about the brain because if you don't know why you do what you do, how will your prospects know what you do or what you believe in? How would you get others to respond to you, or more importantly, would they want to come to work for you?

VISION, MISSION, AND CORE VALUES

Do you think your vision, mission, and core values may affect whether people want to be a part of what you do? You bet!

The goal here of promoting those items to prospects is not to feature or benefit dump them on people; it's to find people who believe in your vision for your company. The goal is not to hire people for a *job*. It's to hire people for your shared mission.

For example, Howard Hughes was recognized for hiring mostly Mormons because of an aligned belief system. I am not getting into a religious precedence here, but I want to point out the culture that he was developing and the people he was attracting. He felt for the most part that Mormons were trustworthy and honest. He was quoted as once commenting, "They're the only ones who know how to keep their mouths shut." He was referring to some of the secret work they were doing on government contracts; it would have been detrimental if they had spoken to the press about this work. He trusted them.

If you were to read interviews with failed CEOs, you would find three themes continually repeated for why they failed:

- Forecasted short of actual capital needs
- Hired the wrong people
- Bad economy

People don't buy what you do. They buy why you do it.

Case in point: A woman whose name most of us know today had very humble beginnings. In recent years, she has been increasingly forthcoming about her very poor and troubled childhood. This little girl was born in 1954 in Mississippi to a single mother who worked as a housemaid. She spent her first six years under the guardianship of her poverty-stricken maternal grandmother.

She remembers having no shoes and being mocked by her class-mates at school for wearing potato-sack dresses. At age six, she began to live alternately with her mother in Milwaukee and her father in Nashville. Beginning at age nine, while living in Nashville, she endured sexual abuse at the hands of extended relatives and a family friend, which eventually forced her to run away from home when she was thirteen.

She became pregnant at fourteen, but the infant died when it was just a week old. Living with her father on a permanent basis after this tragic loss, she began to rebuild her life and concentrate on her high school studies. She was voted Most Popular in her class. In 1971 and 1972, she won multiple pageants, including Miss Black Tennessee, but then she chose to pursue her college education and a career in television journalism rather than compete further. However, even these two goals would prove incompatible, and at nineteen, she left her post-secondary studies to accept a television anchor job, becoming Nashville's first female African-American news anchor.

She then took on the co-hosting of a Baltimore morning show, and after eight years in that job, began co-hosting a show called *AM Chicago*. And in 1983, when her undeniable ability to single-handedly hold an audience inevitably led from co-hosting to host-ing, Oprah Winfrey quickly rose to fame.

Oprah's success admittedly comes from finding the *why* behind people's actions. She aligned with what her audience believed in.

Oprah has gone on to incredible philanthropic activities that have changed many people's lives. She is not undercapitalized; she has obviously hired the right people, and it has never really mattered for her what the economy was doing.

Research in Motion (NASDAQ: RIMM) may be the best example of an innovative company that lost its edge. In 2008, RIMM was the only smartphone of any size and had almost the entire corporate market. But it made one mistake: it failed to adapt its technology for consumer use. In June 2007, Apple launched the iPhone. Its approach is one of challenging the status quo. The iPhone is beautifully designed and user-friendly. "We just happen to make a great phone. Want to buy one?" And the rest is history. RIMM was a well-funded company and a Wall Street darling for a number of years, but it failed to recognize that people don't buy what you sell; they buy *why* you do it.

If you tell people what you believe or what your company stands for and they align with that belief, they will take that belief up, own your cause, and make it their own. People won't necessarily come to work for you or your company, but they will show up for themselves. If your cause just happens to align with their beliefs, they will tell others. They will get the word out to even more people. They will *all* show up for themselves. It is now what they believe, so they will work toward their/your beliefs.

These beliefs will draw your doers, not your planners. You want people who execute and initiate. Not those who continually plan, position, and postulate.

Those who *lead* inspire us. They may be the people who report to you, but they can still lead. They inspire others. Whether it be individuals or organizations, people don't follow because they are required to but because they want to. People follow those who lead, not for those leaders, but for themselves. Leaders who find the key (the why) are those who have the ability to inspire those around them or find the leaders who find others who inspire them.

Our friends and associates (sphere of influence) have an innate desire to help us. That help may be through business opportunities or a genuine interest in seeing us attain our dreams and goals. When you think about it, isn't that what you want for your friends and associates? If you feel you can contribute to someone else's success, doesn't that give you a feeling of satisfaction? Turn your mavens loose in your area. A maven is someone who seeks to pass knowledge on to others. Mavens are your connectors, and if you can find a way to recompense them monetarily for their efforts, you just lit a fire. Maybe that is a couple of basis points on their referred candidate for ninety days once hired. Maybe it is a set dollar amount for a hired candidate.

Great recruiters come from a heart of servanthood. When the person you are speaking with truly feels you are coming from a place of benefit for him and your company, you have a fan. That is powerful and attractive. If a prospect witnesses you trying really hard to align with his or her purpose, objectives, ambitions, and goals, both in and out of the work environment, that is captivating.

The one thing I can't drive home enough is the importance of diligence and persistence when it comes to recruiting.

Most people do want to be pursued and edified. They want to know that someone respects the accomplishments they have made in their career. Let me illustrate this point with another story.

My company pursued a certain prospect for a couple of months, only to have him decide to sign with another company. Out of courtesy, I contacted our business development people to let them know I heard he was going to the competition. Our prospect was going to be letting the competition know shortly that he would be going to work for them. We circled the wagons and brainstormed about what we were missing; we reviewed the information the prospect had shared with us about why he had decided to go to the other company.

After assessing the differences, we focused on what was really important to the prospect, which was strong leadership. After sharing with the prospect some examples of my tenure in the business and some of the people we had recently hired whom the prospect respected, he decided, after all, to join our team. I have had numerous occasions over the years of making that last attempt to cover something one more time that we were missing, and it has often resulted in turning a great hire back our way. In this case, the result was more than we could have imagined. He shared his information with some of his sphere of influence, which resulted in our acquiring three more great people.

ENLARGE YOUR FOOTPRINT

Only about 20 percent of the people who read this next nugget will actually do it. Therein lies the advantage you have over others. The key here is discipline.

Enlarge your footprint here; get to know as many people as you can at the organizations with which you do business. Always have your radar up. Never pass up an opportunity to meet new people. I have always tried to slay an organization's gatekeeper with kindness and find out his or her likes and dislikes. Familiar introductions with your current contact always seem to be the best way to tame the lion. Do your homework on the company. Learn about your customer's organizations and groups and possibly get involved in them. You never know what kinds of relationships, ideas, or even recruitment referrals can come out of these new contacts.

Also, don't lose contact with a former contact who changed companies; that person's moving on only expands your sphere of contacts. There is no good reason to delete his or her entry in your CRM (customer relationship management system). In fact, there's a reasonably good chance the person will become an even more valuable member of your network. For one thing, your former contact will now most likely be more candid about who is looking to make changes at his or her former company or the true reason why people are leaving the company. Keep your network fresh and updated so anyone stepping in to assist you with recruiting efforts is in the loop as well.

There is gold in your database.

If you want your CRM to produce a robust return on time spent, you have to be disciplined and you have to keep it updated.

Never underestimate the importance of people in your life. Getting great at networking doesn't work unless you master what we covered in Chapter 4. With reciprocity, using your CRM becomes more than a discipline. It's a way of life.

It all comes down to being genuine and authentic with people. Most people have a hard time remembering all the details about someone. But I actually enjoy staying in touch with the bulk of my network every year; stay up-to-date on people; there are some people I might not see for a couple of years, but sooner or later, I cross paths with them again. Imagine their surprise when you ask them how they are doing since the compliance audit they went through four years ago or whether their son Mike finished school at Gonzaga.

Therefore, it is critical that you keep an up-to-date CRM in your arsenal of tools and use it effectively. I have met some pretty bright people in my professional career who have amazing recall capabilities, but you can't always remember everyone and the subtle differences that make each acquaintance unique. Can you imagine the embarrassing moment you might experience when engaging someone you interviewed last year and you ask him how his father is doing with his new sailboat, only to have him reply that his father passed away three years ago.

With an updated and robust CRM system, you can be prepared. If you review a prospect's bio before attending a function that you know the prospect will be attending, you can come off as a caring and considerate person, and that is always an attractant. It shows you do care about the person and what is of interest to him or her. Getting it wrong can burn a relationship for a long time.

When I am on the phone with someone, I have my CRM up and open to that person's information. If I don't have his or her information yet, I write down critical points of information that I know are important to him or her for my future reference. I never type it into the system though because then people can hear you typing and may think you aren't paying full attention to them. After the phone conversation, I will enter things like little Johnnie's first tennis lesson, the family's camping trip to Idaho, the person's company doing expansion into a new area, his top producer award for that month, or her new car purchase. This information will allow you to build relationships with people because you have something to build on rather than just surface talk. One of the most offensive things a recruiter can do is *close* a prospect too early. It has happened to all of us at some point when people are trying to recruit us, and it just feels smarmy when it happens. Don't be that guy!

Whenever possible, I try to capture people's birthdays. I will enter it in the CRM system and put an alert on my system seven days prior to the birthday so I have time to make the call before the person's birthday. If you try to make the call after his or her birthday, you may as well not make the call. It just shows you are making the effort, but not really on top of your game. You might mention someone's birthday in a passing conversation, but don't leave the acknowledgment of it on a voice mail after the event.

Some ways to elicit the response you are looking for might be to say:

- "My birthday is coming up. My plans are to.... When is your birthday?"

- "If you were to make a move soon, would anything be coming up like your birthday?"

- "I would like to acknowledge your birthday this year as something we do on a regular basis; is that coming up anytime soon?"

- "We make a point of acknowledging our employees' birthdays here; do you have one coming up soon?

Prospects have a certain expectation when talking to a recruiter of how they will be engaged. Go beyond what a prospect will expect from you. This may be the defining difference between you and the competition vying for your prospect's attention. The competition doesn't suspect you may know more about what is going on at their company than they do. They won't expect that you are sending a fruit arrangement to the prospect's spouse before he gets home that evening to thank her for her spouse's time earlier that day. They won't expect that you will invite his spouse to the office to meet the people he will be working with. Be the gal who makes the recruiting process personal, fun, and a little different, rather than the drab "I want you" approach. You don't have to let the prospect know how dearly you want him or her to be part of your team; just make your approach lively and not monotonous. It's not typical to get married after your first dance.

The items you enter into your CRM platform regarding the things you learn about someone don't have to be expansive. It may be just a phrase that triggers something you know that particular person is passionate about, such as his mother, her clients, his poetry, Martin Luther King, Jr.'s "I Have a Dream" speech, or an interest in World War II.

Take the time to do your homework and then use it in a very effective way by being prepared for your next engagement with that unique individual.

Your CRM system has so many tentacles that run from it. Recently, I heard that a company was going to change its comp plan and its employees were most likely not going to like it. I was able to contact a few people there whom I had interviewed in the past and who were happy at the time and just restart conversations with them. That way, when they became aware of the new plan, they would realize another opportunity was available to them. Giving people options at exactly the right time will have you winning the race before your competition even knows what is going on.

SIX KEY CHARACTERISTICS FOR SUCCESSFUL HIRES

Today, what we look for in prospects has changed. In the past, we focused on a person's skill set, and that is still a part of the vetting we do. More importantly, here are some key characteristics for successful hires to have:

1. **Adaptability**

    All businesses are compelled to adapt to continual change in their environments and at a much quicker pace than we have ever had to in the past. A good book to read on the importance of keeping up with change is Spencer Johnson's *Who Moved My Cheese?* Teammates can't afford to think in the same old ways or hold on to outdated processes that are no longer efficient. Being able to solve new problems creatively requires emotional and intellectual flexibility. Teammates need to embrace change as opposed to fighting it. This attribute is a sought-out trait akin to humility.

As recruiters, some feel their positions have become laborious and repetitive functions that have now just become jobs. It has always been and always will be about playing and winning the game. Top recruiters adjust to the challenges their particular industry presents to them. We thrive off of not only finding one or two top candidates for a senior VP position but four or five because any one of them could make a major difference in your ability to draw more just like them. In a sick twisted way, we get a rush out of it.

As a top recruiter, you are driven to be self-motivated, and you need very little direction because you are focused on winning the game.

2. **Humility**

This virtue can be challenging for Type A personalities. Conducting oneself in a humble way gets you far more traction with people overall than conducting yourself in an arrogant and self-promoting way. When someone can adapt to a situation and maybe even poke a little fun at himself, it is more conducive to a collaborative workplace for all.

As a recruiter, you do need to possess confidence and resilience. But don't confuse those qualities with the need to think of yourself *less* and your contacts *more*. If you are preoccupied with yourself, there is no time for the important work of expanding your company's influence and bringing benefit to those around you. For those of you who feel it all starts with you and ends with you, it doesn't. No one succeeds without the help of others who may be better suited than yourself for particular situations. Get *you* out of the equation.

We have all been in a room with someone who talks about himself or his company too much. How does that feel for you? I know how it makes me feel, and it just is never the right approach. If someone is that absorbed with himself, there just isn't any room left to concentrate on others. By being able to listen to other people's needs, aspirations, journey, and struggles, you gain necessary insight into how you can help them achieve the things important to them professionally and in life.

Being humble is an attractant that leaves people wanting to find out more about you as they make serious considerations about joining you on a life/professional journey. If you read or hear about somebody who resonated with you and would fit perfectly in your network, take every step to make that person a part of your network—no matter how celebrated or accomplished he or she is. Be audacious. Don't be afraid to approach a potential network participant you think is out of your league. Do your homework to forge common ground and minimize the separation between you. The more your network evolves, the easier it becomes because your range of contacts and connections expands exponentially.

3. **Collaboration**

   Success will not come your way without hiring people who have the ability to communicate and work effectively with teammates and customers. Collaboration is the sharing of information respectfully and allowing others' opinions and ideas to be seriously considered. Structured methods of collaboration encourage introspection of behavior and communication. These methods specifically aim to increase the success of teams as they engage in collaborative problem solving. All collaboration requires leadership.

4. **Leadership**

   Great leaders have the ability to place themselves into a situation or problem while also being able to recognize when to retract and relinquish power to the group. At times, you want your leaders to relinquish power to the group so everyone may grow and engage the team concept instead of the titled leader always being the final answer. People need to know the fine balance of when to lead and when to step back and encourage the team to lead. What matters is that your hire makes an assessment of which approach is the right solution for the team and business, and that hire's ability to influence, persuade, and help others to engage.

5. **Hungry to Learn**

   People are attracted to a leader who is hungry to learn. Someone focused on continually learning inspires others to compete and improve. Being able to innovate and create while in the daily motions of doing his or her job will cause that person to fall into more improvements by accident than those who just do their jobs. The yearning to learn more about one's specific job and simultaneously how to improve the company production benefits everyone.

6. **Prospecting for Whales**

I like to explain a "whale" as a slang term for someone who continues to exceed the norm in a sales or recruiting environment. A whale is so outrageously successful at what he or she does that most others pale in comparison.

Prospecting for whales takes far more effort than the typical hire. The whale often is fully aware of the benefit he can bring to a company and many times is very independent. As a leader, you will have your hands full managing this personality and his relationships within your work environment. But that said, a whale can bring a huge lift to your bottom line and set the bar to which your other employees may aspire. A whale can outperform some of your existing employees and sometimes double the output of your current top performers.

To land a whale takes far more preparation; you need to know exactly where you and your company fit into the marketplace, how your opportunity will be a larger benefit for the person than the position he currently holds, and how your offer outpaces the competition's offer. Keep in mind that others know who the whales are out there. You will need to be on top of your game not only to get the whale's attention but to retain him once you have him in house. Whales are a highly sought after acquisition.

Whales are seeking to work with people as strong willed and determined as they are. Do you or does your company meet expectations? You can make a bad hire here as well, so be careful. As much as you would like the whale's productivity and what he can bring to the table, he may not be a cultural fit. I have found that whales thrive on competition and someone else in the workplace challenging them to excel even more. Can you offer that kind of environment? If not, better to fish for something else.

In finishing writing this chapter on prospecting, I had one small epiphany one day when I didn't have my business card with me to pay for lunch. Next time you take a recruit to lunch, try paying in cash. A lot of times, we recruiters are given a company card to use for expenses when we are meeting with people. When people see you paying with your own money, they are typically surprised and notice that you personally are taking an interest in them. Get your receipt, but make it more personal.

CHALLENGE

Knowing what you now know about prospecting, what are some of the things that you will start to implement before you even finish this book that will immediately improve how you have been doing things?

_____

_____

_____

_____

_____

CHAPTER 6

THE TOOL—SOCIAL MEDIA

"Social media will help you build up loyalty of your current
customers to the point that they will willingly,
and for free, tell others about you."

— **Bonnie Sainsbury**

I have dedicated this entire chapter of *What a Hoot! Let's Recruit!*
to social media as a tool to be used sparingly as it pertains to recruiting. I feel it is important to know how to use social media
effectively while keeping in mind it is a *tool*. Anyone who spends
all of his or her time trying to *live* on social media will only have
modest success. There is still the essential side of recruiting that
requires you to go out and meet people, develop relationships, and
be the attractant that drives great hires to your doorstep.

The Internet really came on the scene in 1995 for all to make use
of. The familiar style of drip campaigns for selling and recruiting started to fade into the sunset. That particular campaign was
a communication strategy of mailers or emails with pre-written

messages to customers or prospects over a period of time. With the ever-emerging social web, there is no reason to continue the annoying drip campaigns that get you a quick click into the deleted folder. You know what your prospects are doing, what they are interested in, whom they socialize with, and most importantly, what their interests are.

This is not earth-shaking news, but email marketing is dying, if not already dead. Time is one of the most precious commodities that we cherish today. We consume information at hyper speed.

United States programmer Ray Tomlinson sent the first email in 1971. Since then, email marketing has outlived its welcome. It is not exactly a new technology, but it is now trying to find its courteous considerations. All of the best communication now is about context, not content. Ask yourself whether you are actually bringing value when you send an email. Are you actually talking to your readers about what they want here and now? People know you are asking for business or referrals when you give benefit. The nice thing that happens eventually or maybe instantaneously is that you are the first one they think of when they can reciprocate.

The big thing for you to remember is to ask for the business. Are there any friends or family you know of who would benefit from receiving a copy of my book, *What a Hoot! Let's Recruit!*?

Some of you will take to the following concepts like ducks to water. You have grown up using these social sites to communicate with friends, gossip, and maybe even create a viral experience. Now it is time to put your experience to play in a different environment. For others of you, social media will all be new to you, primarily in two different ways: the basics/mechanics of how the social medium works, and how to apply it to the objective at hand—recruiting!

The thing to remember here is that recruiting is a relationship-oriented environment. Technology is tantamount to efficiency in the workplace and speaks well of senior leadership's vision for their company. It is a tool and just that. The real kick comes from building relationships with people for today and for the future.

People want to know who they are going to be working with. Personal interaction is expected by prospective employees to help them assess major career decisions for themselves. Be aware when using social media venues that unintended friction and misunderstandings can occur often when communicating across generations. When you involve virtual communication, it can be even more challenging. Be ever so careful to use the *tool* with selective reserve.

LINKEDIN

I have had the most success with LinkedIn on the recruiting front. LinkedIn has more than 300 million users in 200 countries and territories with more than half of that traffic coming from mobile applications.

When you sync your phone's calendar with LinkedIn's app, you'll be served up an applicant's profile minutes before you have an appointment to meet with him or her. Simply select "Calendar" from the list of options in the app's menu bar and follow the directions.

When you hear a company is being acquired, moved, or pared down, from the app's menu, select "Companies" to browse through a target company list that you want insight on.

When you scroll through your news stream, you'll see updates from your connections, content being shared by companies and people, updates about the new jobs of people in your network, birthdays, and different segues of opportunities for conversation.

When consuming the news stream, you can interact and add to the conversation when you have something to say. You can "Like" and comment on almost every kind of post, whether that's saying congratulations to a connection who scored a cool new job or adding your thoughts to an article about a topic related to your industry. Nurture your network. Be conversational, but not too casual. Using slang or not checking your grammar will be a turn-off to potential employees.

When you access your Pulse LinkedIn app, you will be on top of what is happening in your specific industry. It will allow you to engage in conversation with your industry peers with fresh information and show that you are on the cutting edge in your industry. You can easily share articles (and your comments on them) to your own LinkedIn profile, as well as to Facebook, Google+, or Twitter in just a few taps. By developing yourself as a thought-leader in your industry, you'll build your network and make yourself a more attractive consideration for someone thinking about coming to work with you.

I feel LinkedIn is more focused on professional businesspeople and laser accurate with being able to identify specifically whom you are looking for. The social network has become particularly successful for recruiters looking for more experienced candidates: 62 percent of LinkedIn job seekers are over the age of forty, and 51 percent are earning salaries over $75,000 in their current positions. Conversely, LinkedIn has also become a vital resource for recruiters looking for college graduates.

LinkedIn is officially the most popular network to find and vet candidates. While YouTube is a great platform to assist as a link on LinkedIn, it is not the best for your primary means of communication with recruiting. Google is a great search engine for general information for due diligence in vetting companies, but neither is it a great tool for direct recruiting.

The value of LinkedIn depends on the quality of your connections. I open LinkedIn every day and spend at least five minutes scanning through possible quality LinkedIn contacts who will increase my footprint in LinkedIn. At the writing of this book, I personally have 2,000+ connections relating to the mortgage industry. You do need to time block on your daily calendar to hold yourself accountable. Keep in mind that social networking is not a quantity competition but a quality contacts platform. A little thing like putting a link to your profile in your email signature can pay big dividends.

2013 was deemed the Year of Social Media Recruiting and according to the Jobvite® Social Recruiting Survey, 94 percent of business owners used internal and external social networking to find talent and strengthen their recruitment strategies.

The use of social recruiting has given us a virtual catalog of prospects who are displaying a brief resume and being an open book to some of their likes and dislikes. It has streamlined how companies find and vet candidates, reducing the amount of time it takes to hire, quickly accessing quality candidates, and broadcasting to a larger audience the opportunity you have available. Social media recruiting has also seen the number and strength of employee referrals compound.

The benefits to recruiters and leadership reaped from using social media to source talent in 2013 alone was responsible for finding 42 percent of applicants, and 14 percent of hires, while the same percentage of hires stayed with their respective companies for more than three years.

Use the hits you get in your extended network to identify the people in your immediate network who know the most promising prospects; then reach out to them. Ask them about the names you came up with and whether they know anyone else who might be a good fit? If you can get them to make introductions, awesome! You can tell prospects they were recommended by a mutual associate.

The ultimate goal is to engage prospects in real discussions outside of LinkedIn. To do so, you can use some mobile app contact management systems that pop up flags on your GPS to show a referral, applicant, or prospect is near where you are traveling. If convenient, it may be a great opportunity to pop in and just say "Hello" unexpectedly to let the person know you are thinking about him or her.

That said, busy people will probably prefer for you to set up an appointment with them in advance. Ask for a short scheduled chat to see whether the opportunity you have available would be a fit for them. When you do get the opportunity for some face time, prep yourself properly by reviewing the person's background and likes to find alignment quickly when you meet up. Think of paying it forward and being a valuable resource at your first encounter.

If you can't arrange real face time, propose an online meeting. Virtual videoconferences give you a chance to connect with people at a deeper level than email or a phone call offer. If there is a logistic problem and you need to get with each other sooner rather than later, videoconferencing is a great resource to take advantage of. Use the online meeting to build relationships quickly. You'll then be seen as a person, not a salesperson. There are many resources out there to use: Cisco Web Ex, Citrix, Go To Meeting, AT&T® conferencing services, Adobe® connect, Microsoft® Lync, Skype™ 5.10, and Brother Omnijoin™, to name a few. Not all conference apps or services have the built-in ability to record your meetings, but I have found that option to be very useful when reviewing body language and recanting specific answers to questions. You can review how the meeting went and analyze areas you can improve for more impact with your delivery, such as learning to pause in some areas and maybe bring more energy to other parts of your meeting.

LinkedIn's built-in advanced search is a powerful tool. It allows you to set a wide range of parameters. Refine your search to the degree of specificity you want to get your results to a small group of quality leads. When you do come up with a great set of parameters, hold on to it for future searches. An option at the top right-hand corner of your search results page allows you to save any search as a search alert. LinkedIn will automatically run this search once a day and email you the results, allowing you to connect as soon as the perfect candidate changes status or joins the network.

Please make sure you use a recent photo on your LinkedIn site. Don't make the mistake of inserting a photo with your dog or one of you on your Harley. You are broadcasting an image of professionalism and responsibility here. Anything other than that is creating an image that is not conducive to a prospect considering your company for employment. I am shocked by how many people fail to include their websites on their landing pages (profile pages) on LinkedIn. People are wanting to know immediately what is in it for them when they are visiting your page. People are also looking at you to see what you are about. Would they like working with you? Do you look approachable? Is your background as solid as theirs, or does your background inspire someone to want to work with you?

It is imperative that you use the settings to block access to your connections. Other recruiters are salivating at the thought of contacting your sphere of influence, and they will do so if you let them. You will want to allow significant profile and status updates to be received and sent to your connections so they are notified of changes. Update your status frequently by sharing new articles, events, and happenings for you and your company. Publish in the early morning or late evening. That is when busy people are visiting social media. Believe it or not, Sunday evening is a time when many professional people prepare for the next week.

Create and be a manager of a group. You are allowed to join fifty groups on LinkedIn. One group I manage is the National Association of Mortgage Processors. By managing who is accepted and declined into that group, I have a nationwide network of processors who are daily adding more connections. You should manage a group that pertains directly to your industry. Let your imagination run wild here. For associations you are involved in, create a group either exclusive to that association's members or to all related persons in that industry. You maintain who is approved and declined. You can send out broadcasts inviting people to your group. Starting discussions engages people to keep pinging back to see responses. With the layoffs over the last couple of years in the processing environment, there is a huge need to be involved with a network for new job opportunities. The job posting section in groups is a big draw to the people in that group. You can run statistics for the groups you create. This will allow you to identify more accurately the characteristics of the people you feel would be aligned with your company's culture. Run promotions and customize those items to expand your presence in the industry.

FACEBOOK

Facebook is another major social media player. Many people ask, "How do I use Facebook effectively?"

Your intent in using Facebook is to create greater awareness for your company. Through Facebook, you can build a viral awareness campaign that gets you noticed not only in your immediate region but outside of your area. You never know who is looking to move into your area whom you didn't even know was out there. By having your prospects "Like" your page, you can develop communication channels and create an association with your prospects and your brand. This connection allows you to build and deepen relationships with your prime prospects and allows them to spread the word about your brand and culture to their friends and other people who may be considering a change.

You can create campaigns in Facebook surrounding the opportunity at a new branch that is opening. Be creative by asking people to "Share" things that their friends can post to their Walls. Suggestions could be "Sassy branch manager needed," "Creative reverse mortgage specialist required," "Homeowners in need of a builder's representative," "Employers looking for affinity relationship with lender," or "Financial planners looking for great lender."

Here is where you can create a point of differentiation between your company and others that may be vying for the attention of the same prospect. It's the little things that count.

Posting videos is the *best* way to create a stimulating and engaging communication channel. Your communication has to be interactive. Through videos, people get to know you and see you, and you create that first impression from a safe place. The caveat emptor here is: It better be good.

Be personal and genuine in your webcasts and videos. Mix it up rather than just say, "I want you to come to work for us." Appeal beyond the real intent here of attracting top people to your company. Offer solutions to underwriting issues, expound on cool marketing stuff that is having high impact, share success stories about production phenomena currently happening, recant the excellent team building experience you experienced at the iFly Indoor Skydiving event. Recall some of the jokes that were told at the dueling piano show your team enjoyed last week. Being direct in your approach is boring. Soft sell in this venue!

Remember to keep things in a humorous light. Humor actually releases feel-good chemicals like endorphins, serotonin, and dopamine in your Facebook friends. That happens when people view your positive blogs, comments, and shares. "Likes" are far more abundant with positive commentary. You are projecting to your audience your positive affirmations or possibly the alternative. You may want to take a look right now at how you have spun yourself on past posts. If you don't like it, you can change it going forward with future posts.

You will need to monitor your page and establish daily time blocks to do so with both LinkedIn and Facebook. If you are daily spending more than ten or fifteen minutes there, that is too much time spent hiding in social media. It will take more time to create your videos, but the key thing to remember is that you aren't going to spend the day there.

There are some great resource links that you can access to enhance your familiarity with Facebook and use Facebook for your best return for time spent.

- Blogs: www.blogfacebook.com/
- Marketing solutions: www.facebook.com/marketing
- Create a page: www.facebook.com/pages/createphp
- Pages best practices: www.facebook.com/facebookpages? v=app_7146470109
- Promotions guidelines: www.facebook.com/promotions_ guidelines.php

Another software developer, Jobvite® Inc., based in Burlingame, California, just launched a Facebook app that allows companies to post jobs and lets users discover and apply for those postings privately within Facebook. Jobvite® uses its matching software technology to connect employers and job seekers through Facebook, LinkedIn, and Twitter simultaneously. Jobvite® also provides the metrics needed to see what works—and what does not—in job marketing and distribution, including views, clicks, and forwards to apply; all metrics are tracked by individual channel (Facebook, LinkedIn, Twitter, and email) so you can follow referrals as they spread across the web. Using the Jobvite® tab in Facebook also gets you to the "Work With Us" app, which allows you to create a jobs tab on any Facebook company or fan page.

Finally, I'd like to ask you please to mention *What a Hoot! Let's Recruit!* in your next Facebook post. It would be appreciated if you would "Like" its Facebook page and post a comment about what you have enjoyed most so far in this book.

TWITTER

Twitter is another major component of successful recruiting using social media. Admittedly, I do not use Twitter as much as I do Facebook and LinkedIn. I do recommend Twitter for recruiting, but you must know what your goal is and be able to direct applicants to a strong website.

One misconception about Twitter is that it's only for young people while experienced recruiters want to use traditional methods because they are looking for seasoned individuals. Actually, Twitter is a great resource for more candidates with progressive skill sets.

As a recruiter, you can use your own Twitter account or use your company's, but it should be clear that your account's purpose is to share available opportunities and information about your company.

Since Twitter gives you just 140 characters to get your message across, be short and to the point. Tweets should be along the lines of: "Looking for ace processor," "Originator's best comp plan," or "Full charge underwriter wanted" followed by "Contact us" at (include a shortened URL).

To make your employment opportunities stand out, you can also use hash tags, which are formed simply by prefixing a word with a hash symbol (#). Hash tags are used as a way to filter and find information on Twitter. By including a hash tag with a keyword in your tweet, it becomes instantly searchable. Here are a few examples of hash tags you might consider using: #originator, #jobpost, #employment, #recruiting, #hiring, #career, #staffing, #operationsmanager, #NAJ (that's Twitter lingo for "Need A Job?"). You can use more than one hash tag in your tweet, but remember that your characters are limited, so be strategic about which hash tag or tags you use.

If your company has a Twitter account but not a lot of followers, workarounds exist for expanding your network and building relationships with clients and talent pools. Run a quick search on Twitter (search.twitter.com) for anybody discussing a specific keyword and you can get hundreds of contacts/connections. You can search for people you know, by location, by industry or interest, by hash tag, by popularity, by time, and many more ways. I've enjoyed building a community on Twitter and following equally linked business development people.

You should also follow associates and other recruiters who might be sources for candidates.

Events can be marketed with a simple tweet, such as, "Please attend our seminar on wealth building through your mortgage on June 15th." More importantly, your Twitter account is a place to inform potential hires about your business. Your tweets say a lot about your company and what's important to it.

Jobvite® has recruitment applications that integrate Facebook, LinkedIn, and Twitter promotion, and it offers several recruitment tools: Jobvite® Source, Jobvite® Hire, and Jobvite® Share. Jobvite's products help with job post distribution, candidate sourcing, and candidate tracking. You can quickly and easily distribute jobs through your or your employees' Twitter network.

Another resource through Twitter is TweetMyJobs. Over 10,000 custom job channels are on Twitter tweeting more than 50,000 new jobs each day. You will receive instant notifications on Twitter when matching opportunities are posted.

A company can post job listings to its Twitter account and then TweetMyJobs will grab them from there. If a company doesn't have its own Twitter account or doesn't want to use it for such purposes, the company can enter the post into TweetMyJobs®' system for distribution. The posting then gets distributed based on its function and location to the job channel. When a job has been filled, TweetMyJobs® will also remove all references to the tweet.

Other services available include Talent Bin, Entelo, and gild source™. These services may or may not align with your favorite social media platform. Select the service that feels right for your company.

Innovation is attractive to top talent, but it requires experimentation with new channels and platforms. Will you be part of the "next new thing"?

Passive candidates (those currently working with someone) tend to be more active on Twitter than active candidates (those not currently working). Historically, these candidates have been my best hires.

When you connect with a potential candidate on Twitter, evaluate the person's activity to see how often he tweets, whether she has a healthy balance between followers and following, how big his network is, and the quality of her tweets. Does he keep a balance between personal and professional tweets? Does she only post updates, or does she respond to and re-tweet others, fully utilizing what Twitter is about?

Finally, once you have created accounts for Twitter, LinkedIn, and Facebook, make sure you are presenting their logos on your email signatures, websites, and business cards so people will know you are on those sites and will look to interact with you on them.

And please mention *What a Hoot! Let's Recruit!* in your next Twitter update.

PINTEREST

I wanted to make mention of Pinterest because it is a growing source for being able to reach prospects quickly. A lot of your competition isn't really there yet in using this resource effectively. However, did you know that Pinterest is the fourth largest traffic driver online? [Source: Techcrunch]

Pinterest is a multi-media channel. Start by using YouTube to show your company in action doing community events, daily interactions with employees, hosted events, educational excerpts, and such. Choose your industry specific material to excite your desired prospect. This is a great place to promote culture, values, and branding. Pin your QR codes here.

The majority of Pinterest users are women. They are pinning images primarily of travel, apparel, and do it yourself projects. Pin your stylish company apparel, pin the last location you had your awards celebration at, pin top restaurants close to your offices, and use Pinterest to your advantage to promote your company.

You are not allowed direct contact to prospects through Pinterest at this time. Currently, it is more of a momentum/synergy building site. (We'll discuss more about synergy at the end of this book.) Because there isn't direct contact on Pinterest, you can redirect the conversation to networks like LinkedIn that are more suitable for direct communication. In addition, make sure interested candidates have at least one way to contact you.

Please make *What a Hoot! Let's Recruit!* your next pin in Pinterest.

YOUTUBE

Today an estimated thirty-five hours of video is uploaded to YouTube every minute. Why? Because people love to watch videos, so if you're going to reach your audience, take advantage of YouTube's power.

Before you begin, however, be aware of your company's limitations. I do my video presentations on YouTube to keep my server and computer memory clear for presentations. Your IT people will appreciate you not loading videos on your company servers.

Practice, drill, and rehearse your presentation before launching it to the world. Being cavalier or too hurried with your presentation will most certainly be met with no response. No, let's call it another word: *failure*. Be approachable, professional, enthusiastic, well-groomed, and most importantly, *be yourself*!

Focus on the people in your audience. What would you like them to see, think, and respond to?

Be intentional!

Keep it simple yet engaging. Again, what do you want the intended recipient to see, think, and respond to?

WEBSITES

Improve your website on a regular basis:

If you see a lot of activity on your website, yet people are not contacting you directly, it may be time to refresh your website. It might be that your site just isn't that user-friendly. You can avoid the dreaded high bounce rate by building a web presence that communicates your vision in a compelling and simple way. If you do this really well, you will make the most out of every visit and your marketing efforts will be amplified.

Here are some suggestions that might help:

- A lot of companies like to link to other sites because it makes their site look more robust. But having too many links—or outdated links that don't work—will distract and bounce people off of your site. Do, however, modify your existing web pages so they include links to your new pages.

- Does the "Job Opportunities" section of your company website tell potential employees about your company's culture, vision, mission, and core values. Do you present testimonials from current employees about their experiences with your company? Do you share employee appreciation events on your site? If not, you are missing out on one of the more important recruiting tools you have to appeal to prospective high-potential employees through your website.

- Instead of the typical HR language and job listings about available positions, your website needs to include some humor, fun, creativeness, and warmth. It needs information that sets your company apart from others in your industry. And it needs to be a site that shows you care. Your job listings should exude personality so a potential candidate thinks, "I like this." And now that you have the candidate's attention, you also need to provide an easy way for candidates easily to submit resumes for consideration for current and future positions. Make your site "user-friendly."

- You might even implement a "Talk to the President" link, "See company video" link, and "Community services performed" link. People do visit these unique parts of your site to get more insight about your company and whether it is the right fit for them. People also do respond to "Interested?" and "Click here."

Website recruiting works and is another great tool to assist your more relationship-based tactics.

BLOGGING

Are you practiced at blogging, virtual meetings with WEB EX, tweeting, effective email campaigns, and using RSS feeds correctly?

A blog (weblog) is sort of a public online diary about you and your company. It needs to be updated regularly, often weekly, and for sure, monthly. It doesn't always have to be you doing the blogging. As with anything, a fresh face, comments, or announcements are well-received. The best bloggers load their blogs with online journals, news, and links they believe prospects will find useful.

Blogging has become the "next big thing" in business communication. More and more blogs are permeating every industry. Blogging creates opportunity. Unlike expensive corporate websites, blogs are cheap to launch and easy to maintain thanks to powerful computer/ remote cameras and audio.

Unlike email spam, blogs aren't intrusive. People want to see them, or if they don't have time, they can make a choice not to view them. If you have practiced, drilled, and rehearsed, then blogs can provide a fast, informal way to share information. They are an inexpensive way to share company updates, industry movements, product-release details, and industry headlines, both inside and outside of your company.

Blogs, like the rest of social media, can be a tricky balancing act to keep yourself out of trouble. By not preparing well, you could embarrass yourself, bore or alienate customers or prospects, contribute to information overload, and potentially draw the attention of some litigious souls. If the blogging community finds out you are putting out poor content, that won't go well for you.

Like any other form of marketing that your company puts out to the universe, successful blogging requires a strategy. The best blogs are lively, relevant, joyous, high energy, straightforward, and well-practiced. Blogs can showcase the company's distinctive culture, voice, interests, and expertise.

By now, I'm sure you have many questions about blogging, such as:

- WHY should we be blogging?
- WHO should do it?
- WHAT should we blog about?
- WHEN and how often will we blog?
- WHERE will our blog appear?

The answers to these questions may vary depending on your particular situation, but let me expand upon them a little to help point you in the right direction.

WHY: What are we hoping to accomplish? Possibly more market share, educating prospects, and developing new markets. Do you want to expose the company's culture or your beliefs? Show them that through personal viral interaction. Again, be yourself. Do you want to promote your company's process or products? Basically, you get to run your own TV advertising here showing how the process works and displaying the best strengths of your products as they apply to your clients' needs. Do you want to provide viewers with news, announcements, and updates? Then show them you have access to information that will benefit them personally in their careers. How about building a referring network? People who like you on your blog will be your best salespeople. They will share your blog with people they know and trust. Then a blog is a great way to accomplish all those goals.

WHO: Who should do the blog? Who is your target audience? Is it you or others in your company? What kind of restrictions need to be placed on whoever it is? Who is responsible for managing the blog? Whoever it is can't accidentally libel, misrepresent, disparage, rumor, or reveal confidential or proprietary information. Typically the WHO is going to be someone in your compliance/marketing department.

WHAT: What are we blogging about? What benefits do we expect? How do we keep it fun yet pointed toward purpose? Do we have a blog "jingle"? Like Barry Manilow's jingle for State Farm™ insurance: "Like a good neighbor…State Farm is there." Remember that one?

WHERE: Where will blogging appear—on individual blogs, an internal site, or a public website? Access some other blogs and notice how you got to those blogs. Place yourself in the correct venue where people will be able to find your blog quickly with search tools.

WHEN: When will bloggers do the work, and when will the company see results? In this day and age, time is a very precious commodity. Travel budgets are driving the adoption of virtual meetings as companies seek cost savings that still permit meetings. You need to be able to show the Baby Boomers, Gen-Xers, and

Millennials you are at the next level already by comfortably using the new venues out there to communicate.

A great thing to do to build interest and set an expectation for people to look forward to your blog posts is to include on your blog a publishing calendar that includes exciting dates, events, product announcements, and new people joining the company and promotions that your company is involved in. You can enter your sponsored and approved success stories here. This further exhibits your company's culture and what you are doing on a regular basis.

IN CONCLUSION

Using social media channels can be a double-edged sword. You can get to a mass of people quickly, but if a mistake is made in your branding or imaging to your targeted market, you can't pull it back, and it is out there for all to see. That is why it is imperative that if you don't have a marketing/compliance department in your company, you must be critically cautious of the message you are conveying through social media. Use it, use it effectively, and use it with reserve, posting only well thought-out messages and presentations.

CHALLENGE

What are three new things you will implement in the next forty-five days to expand your company's presence in the social media environment?

1. _____

2. _____

3. _____

CHAPTER 7

I'VE GOT THEIR ATTENTION...
NOW WHAT?

"I don't talk a lot when I interview.
My job is to get out of the way."

— Anna Deavere Smith

JOB DESCRIPTIONS AND ATTRIBUTE SEARCHING

Not being clear about what you want is the biggest mistake leaders make when trying to recruit and hire new people. Until you have a written job description for the position you want to fill, you are not ready to go shopping.

Writing down what you want forces you to become clear, evaluate candidates, and set expectations—for both parties. Without this clarity, you are just wasting everyone's time.

- A good job description should include at least five sections:
- General job description
- Purpose
- Duties

- Qualifications
- Set the expectation for follow-up

Here is an example of a job description I used to hire my assistant. I did ask for the input of two assistants who currently worked for our company.

Wanted: Personal Assistant

This is a full-time position with an opportunity to advance to other positions within the company. The purpose of this role is to free up Jeff to do those things only he can do: for example, underwrite files, communicate with the borrowers, self-source lead generation, P&L management, assisting loan officers, recruiting top talent to our company, and presenting at local and state associations that Jeff is involved in.

Please note that I have referred to this position as a personal assistant rather than an administrative or executive assistant. This is because we don't want to make a distinction between my professional and personal life. It is basically all the same.

The work can be split between working from your home and working from our office. I will require your physical presence in the office about half of the time. Therefore, you must live in the King County area, preferably in Bellevue. Here is a job description and its requirements.

Duties

Jeff's personal assistant will be responsible for:

- **Calendar Management:** Share Jeff's Outlook calendar, responding to all meeting requests and Bcc'ing Jeff. Prepare relevant background material for meetings and dry run the equipment prior to presentations. Confirm all appointments the day before they are scheduled. Running reports for Fast Track each Monday.

- **Customer Management:** Reviewing and sending pre-approval letters for clients, including how to contact the personal assistant directly for questions. This will be for both purchase and refinance transactions. Scripting birthday phone calls to clients, making those calls, and following up with Jeff on possible business opportunities.

- **Other Communication:** Writing and sending thank you notes. Originating and creating email notes to the team for updates on programs and process changes. Meeting with clients to receive income and asset exhibits. Explaining forms to clients or explaining conditions that are sent by the processor to the borrowers. Suggesting blog content. Sending Facebook text updates.

- **Errands:** Running errands as requested. Picking up dry cleaning. Grocery and supplies shopping for the office. Picking up documents from a borrower who may not be tech savvy, etc. (We will reimburse for mileage.)

- **Organizing:** Working with the onboarding team to assist new employees. Storing and maintaining all of Jeff's user names and passwords. Assisting in planning a more efficient work environment for the team.

- **Entertaining:** Helping to plan parties, grand openings, and holidays. It may also involve booking caterers, decorators, and entertainers, or planning menus and making assignments to our team.

- **Purchasing:** Research options on sales programs, additional computers and equipment, flights, seminars, make recommendations, confer with Jeff, and then purchase the item(s).

- **Ad Hoc Research:** This could include researching possible trips, events, trade shows, information for blog posts, speeches, and presentations.

In addition, Jeff's assistant will need to be able to work well with his team.

Qualifications

Candidates for Jeff's personal assistant should:

- Possess a mortgage originator's MLO license number.

- Be a self-starter, take initiative, anticipate needs, and complete tasks.

- Have a PMA (Positive Mental Attitude). Refer complaints to Jeff and not get involved in negative energy events should they arise.

- Possess excellent spelling, grammar, punctuation, and overall communication skills (both oral and written).

- Be highly organized and detail-oriented.

- Demonstrate a professional appearance and attitude.

- Maintain grace and poise under pressure.

- Be discreet with regard to confidential information.

- Be able to juggle multiple tasks and priorities, without becoming frustrated or irritable.

- Be highly proficient with our LOS Encompass and CRM systems.

- Have a dependable car and be willing to use it for running errands.

- Be able to train your replacement as you move into a position of more responsibility.

If this sounds like you, please email your resume to our HR department at Theateam@hootinrecruiting.com.

I also have seven questions I would like to have you answer with submission of your resume:

1. What do you do for fun?

2. What drives you to do what we do?

3. In your sphere of influence, do you know others who might benefit from an opportunity at our company?

4. How do you manage your time? (Please walk me through a normal day.)

5. If someone at the office offended you with a comment that you didn't appreciate, how would you handle that?

6. Now that you know the duties of this position, what would be your plan to be the best at this position?

7. If given the perfect opportunity, what does that look like to you?

Thanks for considering this position. We look forward to hearing from you. We will respond to your email within forty-eight hours of receiving it.

Now that you are more proficient at networking, it is time to put your improved skill set to work. It is time to reach out to your friends, family, clients, customers, and raving fans. You may have people within your own organization who would love to work with you and your team, but they are currently working in a different department. It is preferable to give an opportunity to someone who is currently working within your company so people know you will promote from within your own company whenever possible.

The alignment can come quickly with people you hire from within because they are the ones most familiar with your mission, values, products, and culture. Hiring from within shortens the training curve and allows the chosen one to hit the ground running faster with you and your team. If, after searching within your organization, you don't find the perfect candidate, then unleash your opportunity on LinkedIn, Facebook, Twitter, and in your personal networking environment.

Avoiding these mistakes will not guarantee that you always hire well, but it will dramatically improve your chances. Like everything else related to leadership, the important thing is to be intentional, even if your process looks different from mine.

INTERVIEWING

The word interviewing is so boring. Maybe a better word would be *relating*.

Your audience—and it can be a group, not just one person—will be much more receptive to you when you are sharing and not telling.

Having a detailed and very specific job description, including the job responsibilities, expectations, education and experience needed, and hard and soft skill requirements is a must have when interviewing. This preparation further enables you to identify the core competencies and characteristics needed to match your culture. You will want to search for someone looking to grow and progress in your organization. Using performance-based job descriptions to define the work, rather than traditional skills job descriptions, can help you avoid making the "bad hire."

Not taking the time here to "do it right" will cost you. Typically, the interview process can include a number of meetings based on the level of the hire you are looking to make. Ensure that every meeting is relevant and purposeful.

You don't want to hire someone into his or her last job. If the position isn't going to be a step up from what the person was doing before, you are handing him back his old job at a different place.

I have found that some leaders are unable, or *unwilling*, to attract and hire people who are stronger than themselves. The best people want to work for leaders who can help them grow and develop. When I have a successful candidate, I make it a point to introduce him or her to successful people in our group who would appreciate having some other tigers in the sandbox. You also may find that the person is a good fit for your culture and the position, but he is less than enthusiastic about the person he will directly report to. If that's the case, check yourself.... Are you making a bad hire?

Repeat after me: "We don't hire friends. We don't hire friends. We don't hire friends." Keep it about business, growth, and objective decisions that are for the greater good. Personal relationships invariably jeopardize making the right decision when it is critical to get it right. Another blurring moment could be not to realize that while your friend was successful with a huge support group with great colleagues, great systems, great brand, and great clients, his performance might suffer in a smaller environment with the light directly on him.

I have made the mistake in the past of hiring people who are planners, organizers, creators, analyzers, and big picture people. I have learned that if these personality types don't also have the characteristics of a self-initiator, launcher, engager, risk-taker, conductor, motivator, and combustion starter with follow-up, I have not made my *best* hire. I have seen a lot of leaders hire people who are competent, but who lack motivation or need too much direction. This happens when the emphasis of the interview is on skills and competency rather than motivation to do the actual work required. Despite the fact that clarifying expectations upfront has been shown to be a primary source of job dissatisfaction and frustration, some continue to repeat that process to their detriment.

"Soft skills" are also vital in a successful candidate. They include everything that is not of a technical skill set. These are characteristic qualities of work done on time, persevering, overcoming setbacks, organizing and prioritizing work, influencing others, taking the initiative, being committed, and coaching others. Other recruiters are looking for these kinds of teammates. People don't fail due to lack of technical skills; they fail due to a lack of soft skills. Hiring someone without soft skills is a classic "bad hire" move. The person might be good for another company, just not yours.

Getting to the "WHY" of your prospect's intention of working for your company is critical. Is the person leaving his or her current company for a particular reason? What attracted him to your company? What isn't working in her present situation? Skills don't predict performance. The best people accomplish more with less. That's why they're the best.

Listening is crucial in an interview. I am talking about a different kind of listening—let's call it engaged hearing. Tune in and focus. Sense the fluctuations, cadence, deflections, and modulations in voice. Women are excellent at this. Men usually have to work on it. Letting other people talk allows you far more learning time than feature dumping time on your part. In addition to asking questions, it's important to allow the other person to talk. Stop talking. Stop talking about yourself, stop inserting your opinions, and refrain from interrupting.

Next time you're engaged in a conversation, practice not saying anything after asking a question. This might mean not speaking for several minutes. Even when the other person appears to be finished, practice not speaking for ten seconds. Often, the person is still thinking, is actually pausing, and will start speaking again. By doing so, you will get a lot more depth from that person.

SELECTING INTERVIEWING TIMES

There are optimum times during the day when people are more attentive and have more energy. This is true for both you and the person you are interviewing. Set yourself and your prospect up for success by recognizing the best and worst times.

BEST TIME: 8:00 A.M. TO 11:30 A.M.

Some people are early risers and will respect that you are as well. If you set an appointment for 8:00 a.m., some of your tigers have already been up for a couple of hours. They are already showing you that they have a good work ethic by attacking the day and all of the opportunities before them.

But I am aware that everyone is wired differently, so what works for some may not work for others. For some of us, our most productive time can even be traced through genetics.

Most effective people are conquering their biggest initiatives for the day early on. The achievers are getting the "Big Frogs Swallowed First." Mark Twain coined the phrase, "If you know you have to swallow a frog, swallow it first thing in the morning. If there are two frogs, swallow the big one first."

For you and your prospect, engage at the top of your energy curve. If someone is interviewing, that person is considering making a major change in his or her life, so it is one of those "frogs" to deal with.

SIESTA TIME: 11:30 A.M. TO 2:00 P.M.

I don't think I need to go into a ton of explanation here. It is pretty obvious that people are thinking about lunch and recovering from lunch. Lunchtime may be the only time a prospect can sneak away to see you, but it is not the best time to accomplish anything. I would encourage you, however, to engage people for lunch to develop a relationship. It is not a good time to sell, interview, or press toward a closing. The exception is for celebration. If you have done the work and the commitments are in place for an employment agreement, it is time to celebrate fabulously in this time frame.

2ND BEST TIME: 2:00 TO 6:00 P.M.

People are able to focus better after their stomachs are full. When the gnawing biological need of hunger has been satisfied, a person is more accepting of engagement around a career change. The small break that you and your prospect took during lunch is a refresher to energy and creativity. You will find a less discerning applicant when your interviewee is not distracted with human callings.

If you have been able to get all of the other hats out of the way for the day and can concentrate on the afternoon scheduled appointment, that may work better for you. You have eliminated all of the day's distractions.

My experience has been that I find myself rushing the interview the later in the day we meet. It doesn't give me the time to listen, assess, and pick up on the key things being said that let me make the *best* hire.

WORST TIME: AFTER 6:00 P.M.

This is when "decision fatigue" begins to appear. Your willpower fades, you make bad decisions, and self-control diminishes. Social psychologist Roy F. Baumeister's newest discovery involves a phenomenon called ego depletion. Dr. Baumeister began studying mental discipline in a series of experiments, first at Case Western and then at Florida State University. These experiments demonstrated that there is a finite store of mental energy for exerting self-control and willpower.

If, for instance, your prospect is visiting you for her second interview of the day and she has already heard about the previous company's benefits, locations, marketing, policies, procedures, vision, education, history, and such, do you think she is going to be listening that closely or have the energy to pay attention to anything you are saying?

WORST DAYS

Two days of the week don't work for anybody: Fridays and Mondays.

Fridays: A previous appointment runs late and gets you into a pressure situation. You or the applicant are leaving for the weekend and one of you has to leave early to get ahead of the weekend traffic. People leave early whom you may need to reference for a prospect's questions. Everyone is busy trying to put out fires. If you see an applicant on Friday, coming back after a three-day weekend may leave you with a fuzzy recollection of whom you interviewed on Friday. The only worse day is Monday.

Mondays: A crisis occurred over the weekend, so everyone is trying to swallow the big frogs first. Your plane is delayed over the weekend and you don't have time to recover on scheduling. No one from HR got the paperwork together and the HR assistant is out sick today. Your assistant is out sick, so you need to handle operation challenges. Business came in over the weekend that requires immediate attention before your clients can start their week. The prospect's birthday was on Sunday, and family and friends didn't leave when it was appropriate.

Therefore, Tuesdays, Wednesdays, and Thursdays tend to be the best days of the week for optimal energy and fewer distractions. Things have been addressed since Monday. It is not a Friday rush. Schedules have been corrected, adjustments to weekend crises have been resolved, and time blocking is back on track.

INQUIRE ABOUT THE BASICS

First, ask the basic questions about the prospect's past education and work history: What is your current production? What has your production been over the last couple of years? How large is your database? What are your referral sources? Can we get your W-2s for the last two years? In other words, believe with validation. Ask your prospects to complete a questionnaire on a source like Survey Monkey® that is custom tailored to your company objectives.

Heed the signals unfolding in front of you. Remove all distractions! If you are interviewing at your desk with a computer screen blinking in your peripheral vision, turn the screen off, shut your desk phone down, tuck away your cell phone on stun, and alert staff that you want no interruptions. You are making assessments and decisions about the person in front of you that require absolute clarity.

When you are interviewing your next prospect, make it clear that you are not hiring him for a job; you are hiring him to share your vision. Does the person clearly understand the expectation of him to join and work with your dynamic team? Not just anyone gets to work here. In the same turn, you as a leader need to keep in mind that people are not objects to be motivated or persuaded into action. People are creative beings, and we are called out as leaders to find alignment with their purpose. You are there simply to present the opportunity for them to grow and be great at what they do.

Every applicant is going to have a little different twist to how you interview him or her, so you want to make sure you are great at listening and reading between the lines of what the response is that comes from your well thought-out questions.

Try something a little different, starting with the next prospect you interview. Instead of meeting in your conference room or office (boring), ask him to meet you in your collaboratory, discovery den, opportunity room, or vision space. Wouldn't it show you are just a little different to your new prospect if your director of first impressions at the front desk announced that Mr. Jensen will be with you in just a minute in the ideas room? Be different right from the start.

ASK SOULFUL QUESTIONS

Now you need to ask the questions that get you to the soul of the person you are interviewing. I have seven questions I use religiously to expose some of the key things I need to know when I consider a new person for an already outstanding team.

1.   **What do you do for fun?**

     Believe it or not, this is one of the most important questions you can ask. Initially, it lightens up the moment and allows your prospect to expound on what he or she really enjoys doing. You will find out what drives your prospective talent. Does he continue to educate himself?

Does she challenge herself? Does he have a wide array of interests, and does he enjoy community involvement and have a sense of family values? Is she inspired, thirsty for improvement, and hungry for opportunity? Drill down a little here. It will be one of the most telling aspects of whom you are dealing with.

2.   **What drives you to do what we do?**

Depending on a person's response here, you can determine whether someone is truly vested in his or her career or just looking for a job. If the prospect is using her position to attain other goals outside of the industry, that is awesome! You can align with that and serve her purpose while advancing your initiatives for a common good. It is not always about the daily discipline of increasing production specifically. Is this person coachable or open to being coached? You will expose her optimism, competitiveness, and need for achievement that she may not even know the "why" behind. This question extracts the person's true passion or the lack of for your industry.

3.   **How large is your database and how do you go about mining it?**

This question is a root question that needs to be specific to your industry. In the mortgage industry, self-business sourcing salespeople generate a lot of business from a past closed client list or referring partners with whom they stay in continual contact. In the new normal environment, it is paramount to be working this pillar of business. If the person doesn't have a database or hasn't maintained it, especially if he has been in the business a while, this is a red flag. Is she implementing a birthday and anniversary call campaign?

Is the person doing her own marketing and will she appreciate what you have put in place? Typically, a prospect will go into detail here about his realtor, financial planners, accountant, attorney, builders, and friends and family's referrals. This particular question is more for a sales-related environment, and depending on what industry you are in or the position you are hiring for, it would be a good place to insert your own specific industry core skill set that you want to know more about.

4.   **Can you walk me through a normal day of how you manage your time?**

If need be, ask for specifics relating to time blocking, marketing, prospecting, file process, and implementation. This question will extract how professional the person is with daily disciplines. Is she organized and methodical with her day? If she is handling a large volume, she has probably learned how to be successful managing a large pipeline. Maybe not?

We all know these skills can be learned, but this question allows you to peel away another layer from the onion to see who is really sitting in front of you. If there is no structure to a person's day, that is not so good.

5.   **The scenario question.**

This is a solution-based question. This question will ferret out what type of disposition a person comes from and what opinions he or she may feel very strong about. The scenario question will pinpoint issues. Depending on whether you are engaging this person as a manager or as a production person, it will take a unique listening skill to determine whether this person will fit into your organization.

You will find out how a person handles pressure situations. Is he able to offer solutions? Can he keep his emotions in check? Does he settle rather than be creative? The scenario question will elicit a prospect's cognitive and relationship skills.

I have offered a couple of scenarios below that can get you started in the right direction for extracting the traits you would like to see.

Example 1: You arrive in the morning to find out that you have docs ready to be prepared and processing is asking for you to lock the rate. You realize you didn't lock the rate and the market is showing a cost of .50 bps to get the rate you quoted the client at par. You need to call the client in ten minutes before the market continues to deteriorate. How do you handle that call?

Example 2: Roleplay with your prospect. Make a hand gesture that you are holding a phone in your hand and calling your prospect in front of you. "Hello, Mr. Low! I was referred to you by Ms. Rate Shopper and she said you have the best rates available. I have four good faith estimates from other companies, but I would like to see whether you can do better to earn my business?" How do you handle that call?

Example 3: If you knew you were going to be leaving for a weeklong vacation and you were going to assign someone to watch over your business while away, what processes would you start implementing to lay the groundwork for your well-deserved time away?

6. **May I see your business plan?**

Hopefully, your prospect has done one. All top performers have them. If the prospect doesn't, that is a red flag right away. If someone instead offers up to you his or her life or personal plan, that also would be great. You just need to know whether the person has a plan. A very organized and prudent person will bring it with him. I don't ask for it prior to the interview, but I do ask for it at the interview. I want to know that one is not going to be quickly prepared prior to the interview. I also learn through this question whether the person is sincere about his career and whether someone else is possibly holding him accountable to it. Is he on schedule with goals illustrated in the plan, and if not, why not?

A business plan can display whether or not someone is aligned with your platform. Lead generation may be something a prospect has relied on, but you don't do business that way. Is the prospect relying on referrals from a builder, financial planner, accountant, or employer? I don't have time to dissect great business plans here for separate specialties altogether. However, Daniel Harkavy and his team at Building Champions are excellent resources for building not only great business and

personal plans but great life plans. Visit them at www.
buildingchampions.com

Some of the higher tiered positions in companies have a
longer interview process with a series of interviews and engagements to ensure the company is being very careful and
selective in making the right hire. Playing golf or attending
a play or professional event together with your prospect
can expose his or her true character and value sets.

Higher and more influential job positions demand that
you hire the right person. So much is at stake that can
significantly improve or destroy your company's direction. It is better not to hire someone and leave a high
level position vacant than to make a bad hire that can
ultimately affect your company's future and culture.

You will notice that I haven't said much about a resume.
I can tell you that it is something I want to see before
making an offer to a prospect, but I don't lay a lot of
weight on it. That said, the items on a resume do need
to be verified. But a resume does not get me to the alignment I may be targeting for our company, so I leave the
verification process to HR or operations. I can also access
LinkedIn to get a quick look at a prospect's past employers and positions held.

I can't remember the last time anyone listed as a reference
on a resume responded with anything other than generous accolades for the candidate. So I feel much the same
about references as I do resumes. They *must* be checked

out, *but* I don't lay a lot of weight on them, and at times, I have been a little suspect of them. When checking references, keep in mind that most people tend to be more positive than the candidate's performance warrants. No one wants to keep someone from getting a job. A lot of times, the reference may be the result of a great friendship that developed from a working relationship. This person may not offer the objective viewpoint you are looking for with the applicant's skill set or relationship strengths.

I will, however, place a lot of weight on a DiSC™ profile. The foundation of success lies in understanding yourself, understanding others, and realizing the impact of your behavior on people. DiSC™ focuses on four behavioral dimensions:

D-Dominance: Direct, Results-Oriented, Firm, Strong Willed, and Forceful.

i-Influence: Outgoing, Enthusiastic, Optimistic, High Spirited, and Lively.

S-Steadiness: Even-Tempered, Accommodating, Patient, Humble, and Tactful.

C-Conscientiousness: Analytical, Reserved, Precise, Private, and Systematic.

On the DiSC profile, I am **moderately inclined** as an **i**. That means I enjoy relating to other people. I tend to have a fairly extensive network of friends and colleagues, and I tend to view a roomful of strangers as a fun opportunity to connect. For more information about DiSC™ profiles and resources, visit www.discprofile.com

Some other great companies to use for personality assessments are Heritage, Strengths Finder or Quadlead™, Myers-Briggs (MBTI®), and Pointward. If I can get a fast track to the way a person reacts to his environment and what motivates him, I have the playbook to find the best alignment for the position I am hiring. Keep in mind that if you haven't taken the time to learn who the people are who are working with or for you, you really haven't earned the right to lead those people.

7. **If given the perfect opportunity, what would that opportunity look like to you?**

You are empowering your prospect to elaborate on what really matters to him or her. You may find that the person has unrealistic expectations. You may find that you can't possibly provide some of the things your prospect would want in a perfect world. On the other hand, the reality of what you have to offer may be far better than he or she imagined. This is another place where you really need to *listen* to what is being shared with you.

You are not there to interrupt or fix or resolve the person's request. You are, however, there to assess whether everything is resonating with both parties relating to expectations, opportunities, and alignment for a *great* hire.

Another key point is to remain objective. Don't let your emotions invade your decision to make a great hire.

Sometimes you can get swayed with someone's attractiveness, gift of gab, or a personality similar to your own. Be sure you are staying true to your plan for the position and the company objective you are trying to match with this hire.

Not asking the right questions can quite easily cost a midsize to large company tens or hundreds of thousands of dollars. Failing to ask the right questions can cost you and your company your reputations, senior leadership their jobs, and business owners their investment. In the mortgage business, you can't afford to make a bad hire because its whole platform is built on earning the confidence and trust of the consumer. By asking the right questions and avoiding a bad hire, you can feel liberated to know you may have just saved the company thousands and possibly millions of dollars.

FOLLOW-UP

After doing the probing and extraction of the key points in the interview…follow up!

This is an opportunity to develop the relationship by bringing up a topic that you discussed before or making a comment on an interesting topic you both found alignment with. Following up with relevant conversation helps to anchor your previous interaction in the person's mind and displays more personality than just sending a message that says, "Thanks for the interview!"

Be quick with information that you promised to get back to the person with. Send the flowers, books, or fruit arrangements. Do all of the things that keep you in the front of your recruit's mind.

Knowing that the people you hire are going to be working with you directly, or they may be some of the people you care about in your company, requires you to take personal responsibility for your hires and do a great job of prescreening.

Getting it right the first time relating to making great hires is critical.

In most cases, hiring mishaps that occur are because something went wrong in the interviewing process. Maybe it was a lack of educating the job candidate about what the position and your organization is really looking for. Is your arsenal of questions that you present to a candidate pointed toward alignment with your company initiatives, or are you just selling?

Another technique very few companies use that I have found to help verify someone's personal traits is a videoconference interview. It is great especially for a follow-up interview because not only does it save valuable time, but you can interview the person while he or she is in his or her own environment. You can pick up on the person's professionalism, appearance, preparation, work ethic, level of confidence, and comfort with using the new mediums to communicate.

A virtual face-to-face meeting may have to be done because of geographical distances. Again, practice and have a very brief agenda. Be respectful of others' time. Keep the video conference to five to ten minutes. If the conference is going extremely well, run with it and empower the prospect to terminate the call.

When I say be prepared for this call, know how to use screen sharing and recording, and have demos, YouTube videos, documents, webpages, and PowerPoint slides ready to go. Have purposeful intent at the onset. What do you expect to come away with at the end of the video conference? Engage your prospect in an interactive conversation; don't be "telling and selling."

Remember to record the video conference so others you know and trust can give you their evaluations later.

"OOPS! DID I SAY THAT?"

Watch for certain words you would do better to avoid that you may unconsciously be using. They can put up walls in communication.

"But" is such a dangerous word. Most of the time "But" immediately tells someone that what he or she just shared with you is irrelevant. The person may feel what he shared with you in the first part of your reply was meaningless and you are discounting what he said. Again, you can offend without even knowing you did it. You are not trying to antagonize someone here. Replace the word "But" with "And."

Suggestion: "I agree with what you said *and* think we can take that to the next level." "And" leaves options and supports what the person just shared with you as relevant.

"Might" is another problematic word. When you are trying to establish trust early on with someone, the word "might" can instantly cause you to lose credibility and sincerity. When someone is looking to you for straight and clear answers and you create doubt in his mind by using the word "might," it shows you may not be the decision maker or you are powerless to confirm a key issue he has. For example:

- "I might be able to get the override for you on your production that you asked for."

- "Do you think we might be able to persuade you to join our team?"

By using the word "might" in your sentences, you are not affirming confidence nor the ability to do what you say you are able to do. "Might" is wishy-washy, and it doesn't leave someone feeling safe with your comments. Show that you have a guiding hand in the process and *prepare* before meeting with someone so you can anticipate some of the concerns he might have. Be direct and firm in your responses to secure the credibility with your prospect that he is looking for in you. If you don't know the answer, take direction toward a call to action to get the appropriate answer. Here are some suggested responses:

- "I am not sure about the total compensation, and I will connect with HR and have you an answer before you get back to your office today."

- "Is there anything else that I haven't covered that would prevent you from joining our team?"

"If" is another word to avoid. When you use "if," you might as well say, "I doubt it." When I hear "if," it tells me someone doesn't know the outcome. He is not sure of the cause or the effect. When you don't put accountability around a statement, it lacks confidence and people know it. For example:

- "*If* you decide to come to work for us…."

- "*If* you were me, what would you do?"

Instead, I suggest saying:

- "*When* you decide to come to work for us, the onboarding will look like this…."
- "*When* we send you the offer this Thursday…."

"When" creates accountability, a call to action. "When" establishes the future along with an expectation. You are a professional and rely on earning your income from getting great people to work with you. Continue building a better you. You deserve it; the world deserves your best. Words are powerful. Use them effectively.

Do you remember asking your parents "Why?"

Do you remember your parents asking you, "Why do you continue to keep doing that? Why are you asking me that again? Why can't you be on time?"

"Why" can put someone on the defensive instantly and have him resent that you are challenging him. I have found a better word to use is "How."

"How" allows a person to relay information to you about the candidate's thought process behind something and get him to open up to you as opposed to shutting down without you even knowing why. A "How" response may even elicit a passionate and engaging answer that opens up more great dialogue.

Suggestions for asking how include:

- "*How* were you able to come to that decision?"
- "*How* did you find the courage to start moving in that direction?"

Career changes are major events in people's lives. They are expecting you to be very good at what you do. With a little cognizant adjustment in your words, you can be respectful and engage people without offending them in ways you may not have been aware you were doing. Having fun yet?

GRAPHOLOGY

Graphology is something I want to expose you to without spending a lot of time on it. By using it, I have one more tool to use that my competition recruiters don't typically use. Graphology is the study of graphic movement.

Although all graphic movement can be analyzed, you need to become really good at the study of handwriting with special emphasis on human psychology. Handwriting analysis is a very effective means of determining character and personality traits. Early in my career, I picked up a very useful book by Andrea McNichol titled *Handwriting Analysis: Putting It to Work for You.*

With the skill to analyze handwriting, you will quickly be able to assess whether your prospect is extroverted, narrow minded, truthful, a good communicator, an active personality, reliable, etc. Something as simple as the slant in someone's handwriting reveals how he will express his real emotions to other people. Here are some examples:

- Slanting to the *right* is to express your real emotional feelings, to be demonstrative, affectionate, and passionate. It also means oriented toward the future. Approximately 70 percent of American adults retain a rightward slant in their handwriting their entire lives.

- Writing vertical shows suppression of your real emotional feelings. It's the slant associated with diplomacy in that you neither express nor repress your feelings; you stay on top of things. It also means you are oriented toward the present.

- Slanting to the left is to repress your emotional feelings, to think one thing but say another. To lean backwards indicates an avoidance of emotional situations. It also means the person is oriented toward the past. The words that best describe slanting to the left are *negative, past, fear, resistance, doubt, repression,* and *self.*

You will learn about margins, baselines, spacing, speed, pressure, zones, and connecting strokes as you explore deeper what graphology can do for you.

A big question we all have as recruiters is: Is the person I am speaking with honest?

When you know what a felon's claw is, which is when you come from a straight down stroke and immediately go into a claw shape that ends, you have witnessed what appears in the writing of over 80 percent of convicted felons. Would that possibly keep you from making a bad hire? So will some of the following examples.

Wedged writing means dangerously dishonest, criminalistic, and crooked, just like the writing style. Wedged writing looks like bent teeth on a saw blade, or like sailboats on the water.

Omitted letters or pieces of letters indicate someone who is devious by way of omission. This is being dishonest by not telling the whole truth. This could also stem from someone simply not being able to spell well. You would apply common sense to an obvious mistake in this case.

Overall, most of the characteristics you learn in graphology seem to be common sense traits that you can learn to pick up fairly quickly once you know what you are looking for.

The challenge these days is that so much is done on computers with resumes, references, contacts, and printed documents that getting a handwriting sample can be challenging. I have asked prospects to handwrite a paragraph for me of what they expect to achieve in a position with our company. For example, before or after the interview, you could say something to the person like, "I'm going to ask you to handwrite something for me just because I don't always remember everything people say and it's important that I'm accurate on this point." Then you can follow that with a request to write whatever you think will help you. For example:

- "Could you, in a couple of sentences, handwrite the reasons that brought you to our company."

- "Please write a paragraph for me that best describes what drives you to do what we do in our industry."

- "Handwrite a list of 'must haves' in your new position and what you expect of me as we consider working with each other."

Just ask in a way that isn't awkward. If you put the person in a power position to respond in more of a personal manner than on a standard company form, that will be more accepted. You might even include a boxed area on your application form where you ask for someone to elaborate on some of his or her personal skill sets that are outside of the assumed and required skill set requirements for the position the person is applying.

NEGOTIATING

I could write a book on this topic alone. It is the most sensitive part of the recruiting process. After all of the hard work you have done attracting, prospecting, networking, and exposing the benefits of becoming teammates to your prospects, it can all go horribly wrong if the negotiations are not managed well. This fun part of recruiting can appear at the interview process or maybe at a final meeting to discuss last details prior to signing an agreement.

I put a lot of focus on the first five minutes of negotiating. In a study published in the *Journal of Applied Sciences*, the first five minutes of a negotiation can predict the negotiated outcome. During these five minutes, the study says you need to focus on "conversational engagement, prosodic emphasis—which basically means you should copy the emotional state of the speaker—and vocal mirroring" to help the negotiations end well on your side. We will talk more about mirroring in a later chapter. I have nine points to follow that have worked very well in negotiating.

1. Always start out engaged and listening intensely. These first minutes are important because the other party is evaluating you most intensely during this time. The person is "sizing you up" to try to figure out whether you actually mean what you say or you're still selling him or her. If you miss any key points, a prospect will disengage here. When you spend some light time at the beginning of your negotiation, you will find the person is more willing to listen to your side of the opportunity you are presenting. You are setting the boundaries for a more respectful conversation if you know you are going to have some tempestuous moments on particular topics.

People who are real pros at what they do know what they are worth and will ask for that right away. Successful prospect negotiators are assertive and challenge everything—they know everything is negotiable. So do you, but do you know the boundaries? Very rarely is "No" a word to be used in any of your responses. There are times when "No" needs to be used quickly to clarify a boundary, but for the most part, it will kill the negotiating process. Always be mindful of "options" whenever the word "No" starts to creep into the conversation. Think differently here and not how you might typically react when you get emotionally involved.

Check your own emotional thermometer before entering the arena. Don't take the issues or the other person's behavior personally. Give some grace to the fact that you don't know what has just happened in that person's day just before he or she meets with you. I have experienced negotiation failure because of someone getting distracted by personal issues unrelated to what is going on in front of him. Stay laser focused on being a problem solver. At the end of your discussion, have you respected the needs of both parties? A lot of times I have experienced a couple of loose detail items before I get a total "Yes!" from the other person.

If I know I am coming to a meeting with a skilled negotiator, I practice expressing my responses without anxiety or anger. Here are some suggested responses you can tailor to fit your style:

- "I know that is something we can come to terms on; let me put together something in your offer for your review."

- "I would like to offer up an option that I believe we can both win with…."

- "We don't have that particular benefit, but I know why that is important to you. Let's consider…."

2. Don't name a figure! Let your prospect identify his current compensation and his compensation expectation. That may seem different than what you are used to. Have your prospect set the figure for what he believes he is worth. You will know you are engaging a great negotiator if his response is "What's in the budget for this position? I can then tell you what I am used to making and what I believe this position could pay." GAME ON!

A number of successful negotiators confer that the party who makes the first offer tends not to do as well in a negotiation. People often underestimate their own strengths and viability in a market. Wouldn't you like to be the one to enlighten someone that he is actually a more valuable asset to your company than he thought he was worth? Preparation here is key. You don't want to be the one being surprised that your offer is significantly lower than the person's expectations. Did I hear you say, "GOOGLE, BING, ASK?"

If you find yourself talking most of the time, you are losing the negotiation. Simply stating your position and then listening to a response is the desired play you want to make. You may have heard the comment, "He who speaks next loses." It is so true. If you state a number, wait for a reply. If you instead follow it with a comment, you lose—every time!

Encourage your prospect to elaborate by asking lots of open-ended questions that can't be answered with "Yes" or "No." Begin with words like "why" and "how," such as "How do you think someone might react to...? Tell me what is missing in your current employment? What does that look like if you win that challenge?"

3. Ask open-ended questions. These questions will lead people to think analytically and critically. By not using open-ended questions, you don't have the opportunity to learn much and you have just given someone power in a negotiation. What you are looking for here is to ignite discussion and get someone either to engage or share more of who he or she is.

Recognize it's not just about the money. (Although it is when you are speaking to Millennials in respects to what's available for fundraising, community events, and self-improvement initiatives.)

Before entering into negotiation, know the person and his or her businesses inside and out. This knowledge not only helps you prepare, but it allows you to evaluate the value each prospect brings to the table in the short and long-term.

A good way to get in-depth knowledge about potential hires is by researching the person's partners and associates. Learn about the people the person worked with as well as the other companies he or she has invested in and see whether you can incorporate his or her previous employment in your storytelling. You will hear me say this a lot throughout our time together in this book. Do your homework! This is what detectives do. Gather as much pertinent information as possible prior to your negotiation. What are the person's needs? What pressures does he feel? What options does she have? Doing your homework is vital to successful negotiation. You can't make accurate decisions without understanding the other side's situation. The more information you have about the people with whom you are negotiating, the stronger you will be. People who consistently leave money on the table or miss an opportunity with a great applicant fail to do their homework.

4. Always be willing to walk away or conclude a negotiation early on. If you don't consider the option of walking away, you may be inclined to fold in to the other side's demands simply to make a deal. If you are not desperate—if you recognize you have other options—the other negotiator will sense your resolve. If a negotiation is going nowhere and taking up too much of your time and energy, you may want to walk away from it. If you appear desperate to hire or acquire someone, you lose. If you are too personally attached to the outcome, you are in a very weak negotiating position. Before you do decide to walk away, stop and ask yourself: "What else can I or my company get out of this situation? Are there other people this person knows whom we might want to have working with our company? Can I insert someone else into this negotiation that we all might benefit from including?" You should never negotiate without options. If you depend too much on the positive outcome of a negotiation, you lose your ability to say "No." When you say to yourself, "I will walk if I can't conclude a deal that is satisfactory," the other side can tell that you mean business. Your resolve will force the person to make concessions.

5. Don't be in a hurry. Being patient is very difficult for Americans. We want satisfaction now. Every time that I haven't cleared my head and focused on the task at hand, I tend to make mistakes and forget to expose a key feature that may very well cost me the acquisition of a great colleague. Whoever is more flexible about time has the advantage. Your patience can be devastating to the other negotiator if he is in a hurry because he starts to believe you are not under pressure to conclude the deal. So what does he do? He offers concessions as a means of providing you with an incentive to say, "Yes."

If you are able to relay the notion to the other party that time is running out, then you have a greater chance of making it seem as though things will be unavailable after a certain amount of time and the more other people may be waiting on the person's decision.

It is a known fact that in the retail sector, sold-out products create a sense of immediacy for customers. Much like the "supply and demand" basics in business, people think that if a product is sold out or if there's a limited time offer to it, then it must mean that it's good. If they don't make the move now, someone else will.

Let your prospects believe the final decision isn't yours. Maybe you have to run things past your HR department, your team, or the company president. Once a negotiation starts, most people want to get it over with as quickly as possible. Let the other person's impatience beat him. Tell him you'll discuss it and get back with an answer the following day. This is also a great strategy for preventing people from rushing you. Maybe you have detected something in the negotiation that just doesn't sound right to you and you need some time to check it out.

6. Successful negotiators are optimists. Aim high and expect the best outcome. If you expect more, you'll get more. A proven strategy for achieving higher results is opening with an extreme position. Prospects should ask for more than they expect to receive, and employers will typically try to protect the company kitty, realizing they may have to be prepared to sweeten the pot a little more to get the best candidate available for a particular position. Keep in mind that a great employee is worth her weight in gold with the performance she can bring to your company. People who aim higher do better. Your optimism will become a self-fulfilling prophecy. Conversely, if you have low expectations, you will probably wind up with a less satisfying outcome.

When you walk into a negotiation, you're not just pitching your business, you're pitching *you*. You may have a wonderful company to work for, but if you're difficult to work with, you'll be hard-pressed to find an employee who will be willing to work for your company. "Build a better me."

So be likeable and genuine. Show the person your best qualities. Convince her that you're worth the investment she is about to place in you by joining your team.

7. Successful negotiators ask, "What is the pressure on the other side in this negotiation?" Understand what the pressure is for the person you are negotiating with. Focus on his pressure, not on yours. We have a tendency to focus on our own pressure, on the reasons why we need to make a deal. If you fall into this trap, you are putting the other person in a stronger position and working against yourself. When you focus on your own limitations, you miss the big picture. You will feel more powerful when you recognize the reasons why the person you are negotiating may give in. Even if the person appears unaffected, he inevitably has worries and concerns of his own that he is negotiating for. It's your job to be aware of the body language and signs the other person is giving you to get to his core issues. When you discover what is causing someone pressure, look for ways to give yourself an advantage in the negotiation. You will most assuredly retain a better result for yourself when you stay focused with the new tools you are applying.

8. Always seek a "win-win" solution by showing the other person how his or her needs will be met. Successful negotiators always look at the situation from the perspective of the person they are negotiating with. Everyone looks at the world differently, so you are way ahead of the game if you can figure out someone's perception of the deal. Instead of trying to win the negotiation, seek to understand the other negotiator and show her ways to feel satisfied. The notion of "You scratch my back and I'll scratch yours" holds true in negotiating as well. If you help someone feel satisfied in the negotiation, she will be more inclined to help you satisfy your needs. That does not mean you should give in to all her positions. Satisfaction means that her basic interests have been fulfilled, not that all her demands have been met. Don't confuse basic interests with positions/demands: Her position/demand is what she says she wants; her basic interest is what she really needs to get.

9. As a life rule, I believe you should never do something for someone with the expectation of getting something in return. Having said that, I believe the negotiating arena is different. Don't give anything away without getting something in return. Unilateral concessions are self-defeating. Always make a loop in a negotiation: "I'll do that, and I need you to do this if I am going to do that." You are inviting the other negotiator to ask you for additional concessions if you don't create a loop in the negotiation. When you give something away without requiring the person to reciprocate, she will feel entitled to your concession and won't be satisfied until you give up even more. It is human nature, like when we were little kids, to push and see how far we can go before getting a "No." If the person you are negotiating with has to earn your concession, she will feel a greater sense of satisfaction than if she got it for nothing.

Be fair—never leave the other person feeling as if he or she has been cheated or bullied. The response from that is resistance. Many people try to ring every last drop of blood from a negotiation. This is a mistake. If the other person feels cheated or bullied, it can come back to bite you—maybe not at the point of negotiation, but later during the employment relationship. The person may not fulfill his or her part of the deal early on, or he may refuse to deal with you in the future. Then you possibly created a "bad hire." Oops! Let's not do that. Be willing to give up things that don't really matter to you in order to create a feeling of goodwill. Most negotiations should leave both parties feeling satisfied with the outcome.

CHALLENGE

What mistakes have you made in hiring? We have all made them. How can you avoid making those mistakes in the future?

_____

_____

_____

_____

_____

Write down how you will pose at least three of the interview questions in your own style and in a way that makes you comfortable.

1. _____

2. _____

3. _____

CHAPTER 8

RETENTION

"I gots'm now; how do I keeps 'em?"

— Jeffrey Jensen

The onboarding process is part of continuing to build more synergy. Just as through the loan process, we do a number of touches to keep asking for the business and enforcing the great experience the customer is receiving, so the same should be applied here.

Too often, our industry misses the opportunity to engage a new employee by having a particular day set aside for him or her to get acquainted with different department heads and key people. By having your department heads meet and spend an allotted amount of time with the new employee, you are showing the new person that he or she is important enough to get executive treatment. This onboarding exercise exhibits a culture that makes sure each person is supported for ultimate success. It should include meeting scheduled time tables.

Your department heads should have a predetermined checklist of items that need to be addressed at the orientation meeting. By having your secondary, processing, underwriting, benefits coordinator, IT manager, programs director, licensing specialist, marketing manager, and branch manager involved, you are creating the "WOW" factor immediately with your new person. Let her know that at this exact moment in time and space, she is the most important person you can possibly be sharing time with. "Not everyone gets to work at our company, but those who are chosen are part of a great organization that just became better because of you."

Employees are most impressionable during the first sixty days on the job. Every bit of information gathered during this time will either reinforce your new hire's carefully calculated decision to remain or lead to "Hire's Remorse."

This time is great for reinforcing trust by showing consistency through departments. The biggest cause of "Hire's Remorse" is an orientation/training program that is poorly organized, inefficient, and boring. How can you expect excellence from your new hires if your orientation program is a sloppy amalgamation of tedious paperwork, boring policies and procedures, and hours of regulations and red tape? Instead, *make it a hoot*!

Tony Hsieh, a Harvard graduate bored with his day job at Oracle, decided with his college buddy, Sanjay Maden, to build a tech company called Link Exchange. They sold that company in 1998 to Microsoft for $265 million. Tony then founded a venture capital firm called Venture Frogs with another college buddy, Alfred Lin. This company was created to fund other start-ups. One company

Tony took a special interest in was Zappos.com, a start-up that wanted to rule the retail side of selling shoes over the Internet.

In 2008-2009, Zappos hit $1 billion in gross merchandise sales and debuted on *Fortune Magazine*'s "100 Best Companies to Work For" list. What Tony and his team of accomplished leaders found out was that by creating a culture that empowered employees to do whatever they thought would best satisfy customers, the employees took more ownership of the customer experience. As a result, Zappos' product lines expanded to include other apparel as well as luxury brands, and the company grew.

Tony is very focused on creating collision moments—situations in and outside the office where employees share great ideas within the industry, but where they also collide with people outside of their industries to create potential aha! moments.

While each company has a somewhat different platform for how it does business, a few suggested items for your department heads to include on their checklists might be:

- ☑ Create Intranet web locations of critical sites for originating
- ☑ Compile a phone list of "go to people" for specific issues
- ☑ Review email program and the options available
- ☑ Use of your Web Ex meeting formats
- ☑ Assign a 30-day coach or shadow mentor
- ☑ Review vision, mission, and core values statement, and company history
- ☑ Present your employee handbook

☑ Share profit sharing details for recruiting

☑ Assign all computer log ins and passwords

☑ Clarify phone use policy

☑ Announce in a local business journal or within the company who is your new hire and his or her background

Retaining employees is just a start to protecting the investment you have worked so hard to acquire. High employee turnover will cost business owners time, productivity, money, and possibly the company, if not managed properly.

Don't get me wrong; some employee turnover may be healthy for your organization, but *excessive* employee turnover can be very costly. High voluntary turnover levels are usually the result of dissatisfaction with one or more aspects of working for your company, including ineffective management/leadership, inadequate compensation/benefits, lack of development and/or career opportunities, and other contributing factors.

In the accountant's world, you repeatedly hear that you can't know where you are going if you don't know where you are. Is your current status measurable?

I have found Employee Turnover Surveys/Exit Interview Surveys generate a very clear picture of your employees' perceptions. It is best to conduct the turnover/exit interviews before your employees leave the company while the reasons for leaving are still fresh in their minds. Time erodes the rawness of some of the tipping points that may have caused someone to leave. The accompanying diagram reflects the process of using employee surveys for your benefit.

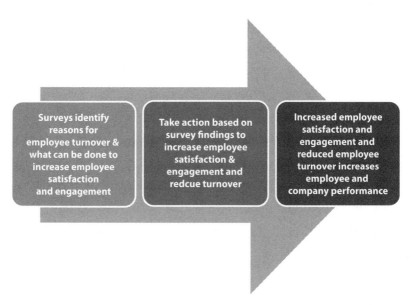

When the economy rebounds, companies aggressively hire and ratchet up compensation. New positions for both sales and staffing open up with attractive growth opportunities. Disgruntled team members and people looking to increase their compensation start leaving for new jobs, which creates more employee turnover. At these times, exit interviews and employee satisfaction surveys are critically important.

Employee retention surveys also provide a wealth of information and insight regarding why employees are thinking of leaving or are actually leaving your company. These surveys can result in a call-to-action moment. You are being provided some keys to reverse unwanted turnover. The little time it takes to complete the surveys can save you big money. The results should be shared with all of your department heads so they can work toward improving the gaps that may be occurring. Of course, if the points are personal or confidential, that would not be appropriate.

Depending on your industry and the products and services your company sells, key turnover analytics and employee annual surveys could include some of the key points listed below:

- Recognition received from management
- Work environment safe and respectful
- Effectiveness of sales performance matrices
- Fun atmosphere in workplace
- Flexibility with time and personal matters
- Mentoring and encouragement
- Competitive compensation and benefits plans
- Leadership communicating effectively and regularly
- Sharing of the big picture with employees
- Support from team members and managers
- Opportunities for career advancement
- Clearly defined expectations of your job
- Job is what was promised when hired
- Availability of resources for training and development
- Company culture in alignment with your career objectives
- Empowerment, Encouragement, Edification
- Your ideas given serious consideration
- Enough job challenges for growth and success
- Feelings of pride in job and company
- Walking the walk with Vision, Mission, and Core Values

- Likelihood of staying with the company for the foreseeable future

- Willingness to recommend your company for employment

- Showing respect to employees and treating them as individuals

- Listening to employees

- Celebrating successes, big and small

Again, the cost of conducting surveys is a small fraction of the full cost of a turnover.

It is critical that you have employees complete the survey prior to or the day of their exiting your company. You need to get to the core of why employees are leaving the company. Finding out whether a competitor has a better attractant and what appeals to your particular employee can prevent a further exodus from your company. If your employee knows of greener pastures somewhere else, you can bet she has shared that with others at your company. If someone leaves, be sure to ask that person, "What could I have done to improve your career at our company?" Put that person in a power position to share freely with no retributions. You are learning here to improve your retention.

Annual anonymous employee surveys are a great way of having people expose early on some things that may be building up tension. It is pretty easy to create a simple survey through companies like ZOHO.com or surveymonkey.com®.

The high costs of excessive voluntary employee turnover include:

- The costs to train replacements and the anxiety created for your customers who experience your new employee's learning curve.

- The HR costs for terminated employees such as time spent for exit interviews, administrative functions related to unemployment compensation reporting, severance pay, and medical cobra explanations.

- Recruiting, onboarding, training, and development costs for replacement employees while pulling current employees off their productive activities.

- Other replacement costs such as background checks, relocation expenses, medical exams, DiSC profiles, and new supplies and equipment.

- Your company's reputation for high employee turnover impacts your ability to attract and hire high-performing employees. It becomes a rich rumor pond for unscrupulous recruiting competition.

The following ideas are applicable for almost any industry trying to keep its most prized resource: *happy and productive employees.* The failure will continue to occur in recruiting if you don't make the necessary changes, according to your surveys, for why you are losing people.

Provide some small perks. You may want to refer back to some of the ideas I shared with you in Chapter 2: Creating the Attractant. Having fun activities, and using contests and incentives to help keep workers motivated and feeling rewarded can keep employees focused and excited about their jobs. I have made a habit of not always making the incentives strictly about the most volume in a month because then your top producers will always take the prize every month. That doesn't give others much of a chance to participate and will actually demoralize them. I try to encourage a variety of other positive behaviors, such as a one touch process for getting approvals, successful marketing campaigns that are measured, most contacts made for the month, or acts of random kindness noticed. Don't think that most production in a given month isn't recognized, but it can't always be about that. Boring!

Conduct "refresh" interviews. In addition to performing **exit interviews** to learn why employees are leaving, consider asking longer-tenured employees why they stay. Ask questions such as: Why did you come to work here originally? When others have tried to recruit you, what made you stay? What changes would make you leave? What are some nonnegotiable issues for you? What is it about your managers that you respect? If you were the owner, what would you change or improve? If you have developed a culture within your company of open dialogue and unbiased exchange of information, the answers you are given will allow you to strengthen a deeper relationship with your employees. The big IF here is whether you openly do something with the information your people have shared with you.

Some items just plain can't be implemented, such as your people going on a monthly African safari. But implement what you can. It creates a sense of ownership for employees and motivates them to help you promote initiatives.

In my thirty-plus years of recruiting, I have found that 6 E's ring true in the different industries I have been involved in. I will follow the 6 E's below with an explanation of how you can be sure to get an "F" in your recruiting efforts.

ENCOURAGE

Create open communication between employees and management. Hold regular meetings in which employees can offer ideas and ask questions. Commit to once a week, or at the very least, once a month huddles. Have an open-door policy that encourages employees to speak frankly with their managers without fear of repercussion. If any of your people feel they can't speak openly, it is the beginning of the end for fruitful communication among team members.

EDUCATE

Foster employee development. This could be training to learn a new job skill or tuition reimbursement to help further your employee's education. Be the source for private companies outside of your company's environment to pick up enriching skill sets. Get managers involved. Require your managers to spend time coaching employees, helping good performers move to new positions, and minimizing poor performance. Encourage communication among your employees to share "something they learned the hard way."

I have always found that with any educational event we have sponsored, the employee must have some monetary investment in it. When people have the event handed to them, they tend to be less focused and feel more entitled.

EMPOWER

I'm a serious proponent of empowerment. Let your people choose to be cheerleaders at work. Let them choose to have a say and make a difference. Let them choose to contribute their best talents and skills. Your workplace will be better for their contributions, and that will be a good thing for both you and your organization. *Communicate your business' vision, mission, and core values.* Display these in key areas of the work environment. Have them be on employees' screensavers or monitors. Feeling connected to the organization's goals is one way to keep employees mentally and emotionally tied to your company. Your team agreed to support the vision, mission, and core values. They own the statements made in those documents. Let them show you how they are going to do it.

Occasionally, have your people participate in activities typically above their pay grade and job description. Maybe have them conduct the next presentation to the group, or make contact with senior leadership on a particular initiative. Have them attend a professional function and be the eyes and ears of your company. Share the power.

EDIFY

Consider offering stock options or other financial rewards to employees who meet performance goals and stay for a predetermined time period, say, three or five years. Also, provide meaningful annual raises. Nothing dashes employee enthusiasm more than a paltry raise. Create a bonus structure where employees can earn an annual bonus if they meet pre-specified performance goals. Look for someone doing something special and promote that in your company newsletter. Support not only the company initiatives you see someone doing, but support his or her community involvement. Recognize somebody doing something right.

ELEVATE

Promote from within whenever possible. Give employees a clear path of advancement. Employees will become frustrated and may stop trying if they see no clear future for themselves at your company. Even if your company positions don't have a tipping point that launches them into more responsibility or more choices, acknowledge significant achievements within that department and reward them for those achievements.

You will find that a general sense of goodwill among all employees occurs when everyone is trying to elevate each other. By inspiring others, we all win. I have found that some of the very people I work with have been single moms, aspiring athletes, successful investors, unknown artists, accomplished musicians, or people who are honest beyond belief. They are all true inspirations to myself and the others they work with.

EXPECTATIONS

You might be assuming employees know what you expect of them. It may seem obvious, but often in small companies, employees wear a lot of different hats. If they don't know exactly what their jobs entail and what you need from them, they can't perform up to standard, and morale can begin to dip. Have your job descriptions well-defined.

Continually changing expectations keeps people on edge and creates unhealthy stress.

Offer a competitive benefits package that fits your employees' needs. Providing health insurance, life insurance, and a retirement-savings plan is essential for retaining employees.

A-players don't have to or want to play with a bunch of C-players. The A-players will help you recruit other A-players. They hang in the same professional circles. They want to protect the culture they are enjoying by reaching out to those they want to work with. A lot of times the work and play blend together seamlessly, and the A-players find that other A-players enjoy doing the same sort of activities outside of the work environment.

Through both intentional and unintentional actions, leaders drive employees away from their passions for their jobs, destroy morale, and often change the team or organization's energy in a negative way. Some leaders had no idea they were doing it. Even leaders who have good intentions can be making big mistakes that are usurping your best laid retention initiatives. At times, some leaders prematurely act without thinking through the consequences. Because so many people are affected by these managerial blunders, and because so many organizations have poor retention, I want to call your attention to these issues and the huge negative impact they have on productivity and future recruiting possibilities. You need to do an at home check here. Do you have the right people in the right places? Keeping the wrong people for too long will be viewed by your team as being weak and not concerned for the rest of the team.

What appears to be even the smallest of oversights—like not smiling or a "Good morning" acknowledgment to your employees—can end up having significant ramifications. People need and want to be recognized, especially your Millennials. If you are focused on the numbers, the technical, the base importance that drives profitability, you squelch the reason why people are working with you. People are human. To focus only on someone's technical or producer abilities is missing the point of why he or she works with you.

I would encourage you to send out to your employees a "How are we doing as a company?" anonymous questionnaire to get an authentic assessment from the team. If you are reluctant to do that, therein lies a problem in itself. The change, if needed, should be led by you to encourage managers to begin purposefully making better choices during their encounters with colleagues and employees so they experience more positive results, achieve real progress, and enjoy greater organizational success. If we take ownership of our own behaviors that might be driving good people away from the organization, we will find recruiting to be much easier.

"GETTING AN "F" - FAVORITISM

Beyond potential legal implications, favoritism has many negative consequences. By not treating everyone equally, a leader is fostering a sense of resentment and separation that will de-motivate employees and damage team unity. You may be overlooking growth opportunities and unique skill sets offered by others when favoritism is in play. When your team members feel their talents are going unnoticed, you will lose them.

When a person or small group is consistently rewarded by friends in management while no one else receives any recognition, it's seldom because only that person or small group deserves recognition. We all deserve the same recognition when we perform well.

I am not saying treat everyone the same. That is not the basis of our free enterprise system. What I am saying is that everyone needs to be treated fairly.

Dynamic leadership (an attractant) will find ways to make sure the reward system doesn't always circle around "top producer" for the month. More times than not, I have found that you alienate your team with consistently rewarding for one behavior. Boring!

When you are creating behaviors you want the team to aspire to, you might make the rewards be about: most creative project, most contacts made, efficiency of submissions, quality of business driven into the company, community service involvement, spectacular customer service, etc.

Display that the playing field is level in your company through consistent policies, enforced behavioral guidelines, valued assignments available to all, opportunities for development for anyone, frequent communication to affected parties, and a *fair* framework within which the employee perceives she can succeed.

When your payroll can sustain it, *hire a Human Resources professional to implement your retention objectives.* If your company is nearing 100 employees, consider hiring an HR director to oversee and streamline your employee structure and processes. Putting one person in charge of managing employee benefits, perks, reviews, and related tasks takes a huge load off of you and ensures that employees are treated fairly. HR managers are also more up-to-date on employment laws and trends. They are worth their weight in gold in terms of the time and money they will save your company. They can set up various programs and perks you may not have known existed.

A key benefit of Human Resources professionals is keeping you out of the legal arena. Nothing is more energy-sapping than the time and energy it takes to defend yourself in court. If you are able to maintain a positive energy toward growing and improving your company, you are far better served than having to focus on the negative energy of having made a bad hire who is now robbing you of productive time.

GRATITUDE

I just recently changed companies, and I couldn't be more appreciative of the friends and colleagues on my team who decided to make the change with me. I know that no one is an island or the end all or know it all. To share a vision together and be on the same page on initiatives is a pay it forward moment. Express gratitude openly, freely, and often.

I have had the pleasure of working alongside some people for decades; we have a seasoned trust level between us. Your/our success is determined by how well you can prospect, retain, and encourage those who are looking to do something great. When you are continually recruiting to raise the bar so *we all* can benefit, you will find your teammates mimicking that behavior.

You may recall that back in Chapter 2: Creating the Attractant, I discussed recruiting like a "pack of wolves." It does work.

HUMOR

Humor is so inexpensive, but when it is missing, work is not a hoot!

The workplace should be fun. Find ways to make work and/or the work environment more relaxed and fun, and you will have happy employees who look forward to coming to work each day.

As more and more organizations relocate, acquire, restructure, right size, and even capsize, our people confront uncertainty on an almost daily basis. The "new normals" keep changing in terms of what they're supposed to do, how they're supposed to do it, and whether they get to do it at all.

The result is often a sense of powerlessness that translates into increased stress, decreased wellness, demoralization, and lower productivity, all of which affect employee retention. We all know people are an organization's number one asset, and losing them costs money.

So the big question for both individuals and organizations is: How do you keep up spirits, continue to work effectively, and maintain health and sanity in a work environment that may be subject to industry and economic stresses?

Laughter is a choice that can be an attractant to any company as well as assist in retention.

One way we can promote employee empowerment is by encouraging employees to take control over one aspect of the situation they do control—how they choose to respond to it.

On days when workers feel overwhelmed, overworked, and stressed, the best human crazy, endorphin-generating, oxygen-expending release is to go find some humor with other colleagues by breaking out the jokes, childlike questions, and non-emotional flippant remarks that bring some brevity to the day.

For example, a way to acknowledge a personality clash in the office could go like this: "I came in today just to see if I can learn from my boss a new way to ignore people."

We all know that respectful humor can put a smile on someone's face, yet a lot of organizations don't promote humor as part of their culture. Coming to work dressed as Big Bird may not gain you much respect, and you do need to be careful with your use of humor so people will take you seriously when engaged in career objectives.

The benefits of laughter need to be more tangible and focused on addressing positive morale, a major factor contributing to retaining valued employees. Humor is a temporary aid in retaining employees, not a cure-all for other systemic problems affecting organizations.

In the mortgage business, at times things happen that we can't control. Rates spike sharply up, guidelines change for a loan approval, a credit score disqualifies an applicant. Humor is one coping mechanism your people can control.

An epic display of humor for the whole world to see was captured during the Apollo 14 mission to the moon. You may recall when Astronaut Alan Shepard hit two golf balls in what many would call an incredibly tense moment for humanity. Do you think that lightened the moment a bit?

With the economy and work stability being uncertain, humor can actually boost morale and reinforce camaraderie among colleagues that is personal and genuine. Laughter doesn't fix the problem at hand, but it does help people cope with the problem. If you set the example in showing humor by leading the way, your people will know it is safe to bring a little joy to some tense moments.

When people are having fun, they will tell associates in the industry, and then, you have created another attractant.

CREATING INCENTIVES

Missing a key attribute an employee possesses that may be outside of his current job description is an error I have seen occur from time to time. Knowing your people and what drives them will keep you in tune with not making the error of overseeing talent that you have currently within your company. The best practice is to offer any new position within your company to existing employees. Otherwise, when they see a new person come in and get a job they would've loved to have, had they known about it, you may lose a great employee.

Wanting a higher salary is the number one reason people get distracted and start to consider a change. As a leader, you may be in a position where an additional employee payout isn't an option because of budget constraints or others in the company who will also want an increase if they know that is available.

Instead, create an incentive based on performance so you can fundamentally show an increase to the company's bottom line; then you can sell the salary increase to the company and sell the incentive programs to the employees. The surprise comes when the employee you are trying to retain contributes to the energy around finding that incentive. For most people, making a career change is not a welcomed event. If they can help create the best scenario for them where they currently work, it will be a win, win for everyone.

You will need guidelines around your new initiative, the first being education so employees know what behaviors and contributions merit additional compensation.

During economic downturns, many employees are fearful of losing their jobs, and this problem is compounded when fewer companies are hiring. When this occurs, most employees are happy to keep their jobs (even if they are not happy with them), and they would rather be searching for a new job if more jobs were available. Dissatisfied employees can become a cancer; they can become disengaged with their jobs, and their performance can tend to fall significantly. This disengagement negatively impacts quality, productivity, sales, customer service, the company's reputation, and the bottom line. Disengagement will poison the work environment. If you don't address it, it will be a negative for your great people who are engaged. Remove the poison. Your teammates will thank you.

STRESS KILLS

Remove stress as much as you can. Yes, we need some stress in our lives to make us take initiative. You need "your best" when you are winning and want to maintain that winning attitude. Regularly set aside time to download some emotions and regain energy. You are on a fun yet draining journey with this recruiting initiative. Stress is a major impediment to humor and laughter. Never lose your humor!

Relax.... Use techniques such as deep breathing, meditation, rhythmic exercise, and yoga. Fitting these activities into your life can help reduce everyday stress and boost your energy and disposition. Stress is harmful when it becomes overwhelming and interrupts the healthy state of equilibrium that your nervous system needs to remain in balance. Overwhelming stress is an increasingly common characteristic of our lives today. Relaxation controls the anxiety and heightened state of readiness you are experiencing and calms your mind into a state of equilibrium.

Some things are so simple to do, and it doesn't cost you anything simply to give yourself a mental health break. Just try purposeful deep breathing the next time you are feeling stress. I do this before I speak at an event to calm my mind. I will do this standing up or sitting down.

I breathe deeply from the abdomen, injecting as much fresh air as possible into my lungs. I will inhale through my nose while placing my hand on my abdomen to feel the rise as I am inhaling. Exhale through your mouth while contracting your abdominal muscles. By keeping your hand on your abdomen, you will stay more focused on registering whether your abdomen is contracting. I continue doing this to the count of ten. That little break is remarkable.

COMMUNICATION, COMMUNICATION, COMMUNICATION...

I am talking about being deliberate with effective communication that your team is desperate for. People left to their own assumptions will typically not be accurate in their assumptions. That is your fault if you are not communicating. If you and your team are going to be effective leaders, you must be deliberate in keeping your team informed. Lack of information will create stress and mistrust for those who are looking for you to be transparent and informational. During times of disruption in your organization, even when good disruption is occurring, such as *growth*, you need to step up the communication.

Some key advantages to incorporate regularly and especially during disruptive times in your company are:

- Write the announcement down and review it. Does it sound inclusive and all-encompassing in its nature? If there are things that can't be answered just yet, state that and the "Why" behind it.

- Prior to making any announcement, contact key influencers in your organization so they can be prepared to answer questions that subordinates will have. This will show a consistent message and relieve people's fears because the leaders are aligned and things have been well thought-out. Make sure you have alignment with your leadership team so it fully understands before you make any disruptive announcement.

- Announce any changes that will affect your people as soon as you are prepared and have walked through the change in your mind from A to Z. Delays create anxiety for everyone.

- Set the expectation of being available for any and all questions that the announcement may have caused concerns about or didn't completely address. Direct communication and availability with both supervisors and executive management is preferred. This communication conveys to your people that they are recognized and important. As leaders, our time is full and precious, and we are trying to accomplish great things during the day too. A leader's main job is to support the success of all of his or her reporting employees. That is the key to our own success.

- Implement and do what you say you are going to do.

In my career, I have witnessed a number of situations where communication would have been the simple solution as opposed to the disaster that truly occurred.

TRAINING

Training is not…a periodic announcement that goes out on an email that announces a 9:00 a.m. mandatory training tomorrow. Nor is training making people sit through PowerPoint slides, graphs, and drone data. Meetings should have expectations established weekly/ monthly/quarterly so people can count on a consistent schedule. Say up front what the topic is—for example, the workflow process.

Training should "look, feel, and taste" like direct Positive Professional Development and Skills Enhancement! The content and learning components have to be seen to improve an individual's skills—actually, his or her range of value!

Start designing the training you need to improve, introduce, grow, or launch a new initiative. Focus on what you are trying to accomplish. The key component will be to answer "What's in it for your people?" They need to see clearly what the benefit is and that it is clearly understood. Ensure that there is a strong "What's in it for *me*?" training benefit that is clearly seen and understood.

Everyone learns something from training, even if that learning is totally opposite to the intent.

A couple of points of contention I have encountered in setting up trainings in the past are:

- People get upset that the training was scheduled at such short notice.

- Their day has been disrupted—they are extremely busy right now.

- What they will learn is how much behind they are when the session is over.

- The top sales producers consider the training a repeat event.

From a company viewpoint, training is a learning experience needed for effective professional development and skills enhancement that will greatly elevate the significance and retention quality of the people exposed to the training. The anticipated result is that the training will directly contribute to time effectiveness, significant cost savings, and measurably elevated contributions to the company's bottom line. Retention of employees will be greatly increased.

Through training, not only are we seeking a return on investment for our company as a whole, but specifically, we want our employees acting as a "pack of wolves" from the recruiting side for their skill enhancement. The training you provide will present the opportunity and knowledge for hiring managers to develop and strengthen the necessary skills (creating the attractant, networking, prospecting, and developing momentum) to gain, maintain, and advance in their own professions.

From a salesperson's viewpoint, your training must include and deliver training for all your producers that clearly can be seen as personal development and skill enhancement. The items included need to be so important that if employees miss them, they could be missing their edge over their competition. Training should potentially ensure that a top producer will be more productive and more rewarded in his or her career and monetarily. Keep in mind the "What's in it for *me?*" skills enhancement need from the salesperson's perspective!

Effectiveness can be greatly improved with just a little bit of thought and practice. Using a candidate-centric approach will help you structure your thoughts and provide a place for practice. As a result, you will have an increased chance to recruit and retain the best candidate for your team.

Professional development isn't a one-time event; it is a continuous part of your role as a hiring manager. Make it your priority to assess and improve your own skill sets and enhance the skills of your team, and then watch how you increase your value to your team and the entire organization.

Through training, a person can improve his overall performance in any identified area, and in doing so, can improve the overall quality of his life. Professional development typically uses a combination of cognitive and behavior problem-solving approaches, both of which are used to strengthen a person's positive skill development (personal and professional).

You may very well be the recruiter and professional trainer in your organization. In that case, *you* will want to be prepared for the training. When done right, your employees will own becoming recruiters and trainers themselves.

Be creative with your training. Make it a Hoot!

There are the more integral training programs you will put together that are company and industry specific, and then there is the fun stuff as a distraction, such as marketing outrageously, negotiating the deal, effective imagination, rallying the whales, and learning the birth orders; just be creative and have some fun with it.

If you do not have an internal training team, then you need to get an outside vendor to help you. If you do a little "homework," you will soon discover that leading industry training vendors have the "cream of the crop" in people, experience, curriculum, and delivery credibility to make training your secret weapon in the recruiting and retention wars!

Make certain that the training vendor you select has skill set courses that are developed and delivered by subject-matter-experts who really know your industry's business and your industry's timely marketplace in detail. Use the tools you learned about in the social media chapter to research and expand your knowledge about the vendor's expertise within your particular industry.

A reputable vendor is not as expensive as you might think. The time and money an outside vendor will save you as well as materials, personnel, and planning are considerably less expensive at times than trying to do it in house. If a training vendor will not listen to your customizing needs, cross it off the list! Next!

THE COUNTER OFFER

This is the position no one likes to be in. Someone who currently works with you has presented a resignation letter to you. All of the investment, all of the promise this person has shown, and all of the time you have poured into this person is now about to walk out the door. Ugh!

I am not talking about the person whom you are relieved has quit on his or her own. This is someone you don't want to lose.

As with negotiating, the next gestures, comments, and reactions can either give you a chance at retaining this person or you can be faced with a loss.

Realize that the person standing before you is emotional, nervous, and anticipating your reaction. Do you remember the last time you tendered a resignation? Doing so is nerve racking.

Accept the resignation letter graciously and with an inquisitiveness that will surprise that person. Do not bio react or make any direct comment or "you" statements. (Remember, we discussed bio reaction in Chapter 5.) *Do* express your disappointment, comment on what the person has meant to you and your company, and thank the person for his or her service. Wish the person well and stop there.

You may be thinking, "Is that it?" regarding this advice. Yes!

This feels brazen and like you are closing the table for further discussion. You have just removed any defenses the person may have prepared to justify his or her reason for resigning.

The next day when your friend/employee is feeling relieved and beginning to settle with the resignation, have someone else reach out to him—someone the person trusts, such as your direct report or the company president. If you are the president, maybe your wife. Have the person express shock and disappointment, not in the person, but in the fact that your company is about to lose a great person and teammate.

That concerned call can go something like "Sandy, we all want to know what is going on with your present situation? How can I/we help you?" It can't be anything other than genuine concern for that person. This person's responses are not to be challenged. You will need to coach the person you have appointed to insert herself into the situation on how to manage the interaction with your person you want to stay on your team.

This safe and open environment should empower the employee to speak directly about the issues that moved the employee to this place. Your employee's emotions and core issues will emerge. Once the core issues have been exposed, just make a note of them. Refrain from "fixing the problem" on that call. You and the employee will be better served by continuing the conversation about the positive attributes of his current job or company. If there is hope of retaining this valuable employee and he feels a genuine effort is being made to correct or stabilize his issues, therein lies your hope for retaining this employee. In some cases, issues just can't be resolved, so it is best to agree there is just not a way to resolve the lack of job advancement, personality differences, new locations being sprung, or educational benefits, and the person does just need a change.

It may be enough that someone is feeling heard and his work is being recognized or that there is a monetary increase or a department is morphed to fit a more conducive work environment. This can also be an opportunity to learn more about some of the challenges that the other employees are facing that you can get corrected before losing more people over some of the same issues. Win-Win!

In your counteroffer, be considerate of the fact that simply offering more money can actually be an insult and raise the question "Were you knowingly taking advantage of me the whole time and not rewarding my efforts until I said something?" Ugly, Uglier, and Ugliest!

You hope that you don't get into a position like this very often, but now that you are learning to make every experience in the recruiting environment a positive learning opportunity, you and others will benefit from your changed attitude.

TERMINATION

It may seem odd to end a chapter on retention by addressing termination. It's a tough decision to let someone go from your company. Sometimes, the decision is affected by personal pride because you hired someone you saw potential in, and you invested your time, energy, and money into that person, but it just hasn't worked out. Face it…you made a bad hire.

When you get to the point of making the decision to terminate, don't wait too long. You know you may have given the person one too many second chances already; you tried to get someone to learn at his own pace, and you stayed positive until even you had no patience left. Now you are aggravated and realize that you should have terminated him months ago.

Below, I have listed some things to validate your decision and empower you to terminate. I also want to expose some collateral damage that prolonging the decision can do in this situation:

- The person who needs to be terminated has probably already harmed the company morale and culture, not to mention he's probably miserable himself. How's that? At the point you let him go, the employees who work directly with him may be beyond aggravated. Your great people will leave. Your employees will have doubts about your leadership skills. Your peers and subordinates may lose trust in your decision-making.

- You might think the person to be terminated may cost you more time in trying to replace the tasks he was completing, although it was short of what the position called for. I have found that other people are just waiting for the opportunity to advance and give it a go in that position. You probably have an amazing person in the company ready to advance or take on a few more responsibilities to challenge her a little more. It does add some new juice to the team.

- You might think it will be an unpopular decision to let go of the person who needs to be terminated. You can't be afraid that everyone will leave if this person is terminated. In most cases, your employees will thank you and will most likely respect you for taking charge. A quick reality check with peers will tell you that, in fact, everyone doesn't love him. People will work with you and your business because they like you and what they do. Removing someone from the equation who is a negative distraction will improve morale.

Anyone who is holding up the momentum of your company doesn't belong there.

CHALLENGE

What are three takeaways you can implement this month that will improve your retention percentages? They may not cost you anything monetarily; it might just be a change in process or an acknowledgment of an area you had been overlooking that can be changed pretty quickly.

1. _____

2. _____

3. _____

CHAPTER 9

MOMENTUM

"We have lift-off!"

— NASA

It is time to *ignite* your spark. You are the igniter—someone who really cares about people and their futures—someone who is willing to invest and believe in people. Make yourself available to the cause. By igniting others, I have found it ignites and inspires me. When you align with the *why* others have a passion for, you have lift off!

No matter what type of business or organization you lead, or what kind of personal and business goals you are pursuing, one of the markers that will determine your level of success is momentum. However, momentum can often feel fleeting; something that seems to be here today and yet is gone tomorrow.

At this stage in the recruiting cycle, a diversity of opinions, ideas, and experiences is incredibly valuable. Be listening closely for beneficial advice from others here. Team chemistry perpetuates with team diversity, and other team players will balance each other out. I love the mishmash of ideas that when collaborated on, energizes the group as a whole. *We* can do it! *I* can't do anything! Diversity always overcomes adversity.

In his wonderful book *Musicophilia*, neurologist Oliver Sacks describes Clive Wearing, a musician and musicologist whose memory was erased almost entirely after a severe brain infection. In fact, Jocelyn Glei of 99u.com shared with me that post-trauma, Clive's short-term memory lasted only a matter of seconds.

Sacks writes, "He remembers almost nothing unless he is actually doing it, then it may come to him." Yet Clive's musical self, his *performative* self, remained almost completely intact. It just needed to be activated. When playing music or conducting a choir, Clive could reattain his former virtuosity. As long as his fingers and his mind were in motion, he could play beautifully. Clive's wife writes, "The momentum of the music carried Clive from bar to bar…. He knew exactly where he was because in every phrase there is context implied, by rhythm, key, melody…. When the music stopped, Clive fell through to the lost place. But for those moments he was playing he seemed normal."

We are perhaps not so different from Clive when it comes to creative projects. The minute that we lose momentum, we lose the thread. We become extremely vulnerable to distraction and defeat. Our inner critic awakens, and we start second-guessing ourselves, doubting the possibility of success. Other people's demands creep in, vying for our attention and focus. We start to generate shiny, new ideas that seem even more worthy of execution, tempting us to move onto *the next big thing* without ever finishing the task we set out on.

The minute we lose momentum, we lose the thread.

It's just like Newton's First Law of Motion: The tendency of a body in motion is to keep moving; the tendency of a body at rest is to sit still. In other words, it's a lot less work to keep moving once you have some momentum than it is to start moving from a dead stop.

If we can keep moving on our projects every day—stoking that creative fire regularly to keep the flames high—it's infinitely easier to stay focused, make great strides, and blast through the roadblocks that inevitably come up. You will be rewarded with a consistent feeling of progress; and, most importantly, it keeps the ball moving forward. The time blocking that you have learned in previous chapters is paramount here. Even if you're working on recruiting for just an hour a day, that's enough to keep your objectives and recent activities fresh.

You are going to encounter necessary distractions some days that are going to take you off course. But if you're striving, executing, and time blocking to push it forward every single day, you'll stay on track regardless.

You begin to feel momentum when you burst through objections in your path like they were tissue paper. Momentum is when goals are reached relatively easily, one success follows another, and forward growth comes quickly. Momentum allows leaders to move through setbacks quickly, and any kind of adjustment is possible. Your people throughout the organization are motivated to achieve more on their own and with more energy.

CAUTION

A false sense of security can be dangerous. Sustaining a successful business is a matter of discipline, and staying hungry is half the battle. Don't let your recent successes make you complacent and even a little cocky.

If you're in sales, momentum is when you are more confident and sales become easier. As a recruiter, more people are reaching out to contact you and the prospecting doesn't seem to be as intense on your end. You will find the momentum overflowing into your personal life. Momentum happens when your life is in balance and everything is going right. Be patient, prepare, and continue to plant seeds. You are about to be rewarded for your efforts again. Keep in mind that the balance we are trying to maintain doesn't mean hours worked. It does, however, mean being efficient, productive, and selective. Measure yourself by the results, not the hours worked.

Nothing feels better than winning. But while you are basking in the proceeds of that big commission check, or relaxing on the beach at your national sales award trip, ask yourself this question: What's next?

You see, winning was a challenge. It required perseverance, training, hard work, and focus. But all too often, after achieving our big goals, we take our foot off the pedal and have a tendency to coast for a while. Relaxing in the glow of our victory, we quickly forget that the game is still on. Our competitors are not resting; instead, they are motivated and synergized by the new level we have just set.

I love the single word *synergy*. Merriam-Webster defines it as: the increased effectiveness that results when two or more people or businesses work together.

When we rest on our laurels, that's where *inertia* can occur. Inertia is defined as: An object in motion tends to stay in motion, and an object at rest tends to stay at rest. Be aware that you can fall into a state of euphoria, which when indulged too long, you may find hard to escape from. By recognizing this state of mind occurring within you or better yet preventing it from occurring, you will be in a far better place to maintain momentum. Prior to reaching your goals, discipline yourself to ask again, "What's next?" Then you will find that your successes will create the synergy you need to propel you into your next achievement. Celebrate your achievements; just don't live there.

Momentum starts with you, the leader. Your team will feel the synergy as it moves outward and impacts the entire team. Your team's momentum starts with your personal momentum. You need to be motivated and moving forward yourself before you can encourage others. It is okay to encourage friendly competition among your team members. I continually offer incentives based on measurable results, and then I stand back to watch my team members self-manage and push each other to accountability goals that they achieve together.

Even if your business has been around a long time, you or your business development team has fallen off the recruiting pace, you have had to regroup as a result of downsizing, or you have had to readjust processes, you can restart your momentum. There is no better day than today and tomorrow. What are you doing with your 86,400 seconds that you will be given tomorrow?

You could start by making a massive amount of prospecting calls to bring in a large number of new prospects. Start creating momentum by doing massive amounts of what it takes to succeed. It's important to set small, realistic goals at first. Challenge yourself, but don't try to do too much and stop before you ever get going. Set achievable goals, and experience incremental success to help you build momentum and confidence.

Continue to build momentum when setting an appointment with a prospect. The best time to make a new prospecting call is immediately after you just set your next appointment. Too many people will stop and take a break after they meet some goal or objective. When your competition thinks it deserves a reward, it takes a break. If you take a break after each small success, you're robbing yourself of the momentum you can achieve. You have just beat a deadline and gained a tremendous amount of energy and confidence from that action—so take advantage of it and make the next step. I am sure you are most motivated immediately following a success, so make use of that motivation to continue the forward motion you've started. Reward yourself later; the competition is hoping you will rest!

When they witness their success, your employees and business development team will feel their motivation rising. You can capitalize on this feeling by putting them in situations that allow them to see some wins in what they are doing. Look for any way you can of helping them succeed. The more wins they can have, the more confidence they will have and the more momentum they will be helping you to build.

IGNITE YOUR MOMENTUM!

Most successful people created their own "luck," and you need to know when to take advantage of that "luck."

You are now in a place to replicate, broadcast, and expand your footprint!

Continue pursuing collaborative discussion among your team and brainstorm about your next steps. Identify market areas where you want to expand so you can recruit from them. At the same time, identify areas where you may want to expand your company. Do your homework about the metrics and demographics of the area. The information-gathering stage is for brainstorming followed by a freewheeling discussion to analyze the ideas.

After you have this data plan, determine whom you will have on your support groups before launching into those areas. Discuss preparation and participation and define your purpose for this discussion. Developing a synergistic recruiting team environment with rich collaborative discussion and brainstorming is not easy; it will, however, provide rich rewards both in personal satisfaction and your recruiting success.

The challenge now is to create a cohesive team environment where *everyone* is participating and feels comfortable sharing his or her ideas and opinions. If any one team member doesn't share her idea or opinion because she feels uncomfortable or not heard, it limits the possibility of a synergistic solution. *Elevated discussion can be a good thing as long as it is not meant to intimidate and it focuses on the ideas for recruiting.* When the discussion turns toward people, typically that is not constructive. This diverging discussion is only valuable as long as it is leading to a collaborative solution to recruiting or the decision at hand. When the discussion begins to get redundant and/or a synergistic solution begins to emerge, it is time to move to the closing stage. At this point, the discussion becomes much more calculated and focuses on converging on an outstanding decision or the issue's resolution. Discussion, brainstorming, and synergy can lead to an outstanding leadership team that develops great synergistic solutions. Leadership/recruiting teams need a few rules and some structure to be highly effective. Diversity is a great asset here as long as there is a common purpose. Here are some guidelines for creating an effective team:

1.   **Define team responsibilities and roles:** What will we be accomplishing by the end of this discussion? What roles will be required, and who will take on those roles? Who's responsibility is it to speak up if the discussion is flailing? Is that same person in charge of moving the discussion along? Who records or documents the progress and notable ideas? Who implements the synergistic solution? Who oversees that the comments are relevant and constructive to the discussion's purpose?

2.   **Set performance rules:** Don't be late and start on time. Start and end the discussion at the times prearranged. Be respectful of each other's time and have a printed agenda. Be courteous to the person speaking and see that his or her ideas are given the full time needed to present.

3.   **Determine which decisions are the team's responsibility:** Who writes the agreements? Who makes the offer?

Who takes the next step with a prospect? Who coordinates the onboarding? Who sends the interview follow-up items? Who does the prospecting? What resources are we using for prospecting, and who is responsible for follow up?

Finally, when ending a discussion, make a practice of summarizing the salient points and takeaways, making sure all participants know precisely what actions will be taken and by whom. I've also found it helpful to offer a last opportunity for anyone in the room to speak up by asking, "Is there anything else?" or "What have we missed?" Often, someone has wanted to say something important but never found the opportunity until then.

Hopefully, when a discussion does end, it has been valuable enough that people look forward to the next one.

Developing a synergistic leadership team environment must be a priority and a focus. It also may require outside expertise. I have at times been involved with contract leadership companies that bring an outside viewpoint to the planning processes; this outside evaluation has worked out very well.

With synergy and growth comes reluctance by some and downright resistance from others. In the book *Who Moved My Cheese?*, Spencer Johnson speaks about how "movement in a new direction helps you find new cheese." One of his characters discovers how finding new venues nourishes his soul. Moving in a new direction freed the character from old habits and was like a cool breeze blowing in his face; taking deep breaths in this cool breeze invigorated him. We are called to move in a new direction as well once we have created synergy and want to sustain the momentum behind it.

My most recent experience with creating synergy has been with the Mortgage Advisory Group. For eight months, I didn't have much lift, but through persistently implementing the five steps, we went from eight people in the office to twenty-eight—a 71 percent increase in one year. Once we gained momentum, we replicated it. We opened a Woodinville branch and we hired managers for the Issaquah, Kirkland, and Vancouver branches; we were even looking forward to opening a Seattle branch. Suddenly, we heard people saying things like:

- "What are you guys doing over there?"
- "We are hearing good things about your company."
- "I heard you just hired...."
- "It seems like we are seeing you everywhere."
- "How would you like to serve on this board?"
- "Can I talk with you about...?"

When this kind of momentum happens, it is not the time to rest; it is the time to capitalize, grow, and continue your momentum. It is the break point where you ride the wave and reap the rewards of your well-planted seeds.

As your transformation occurs, also be aware of the great hires you have made. When you originally interviewed them, they showed that they had a higher calling. They had a particular purpose they wanted to serve by coming to your company. That purpose may have been to change lives, change your industry, or change themselves in a positive way. If you are a transformational leader, you will remember, recognize, and respond to what your people need to achieve their purposes.

Your work group will show a contagious spirit about having everyone excel. It will change lives. That is one of the attractants you are seeking, and it is more important than the work at hand itself. People yearn to be a part of something successful and affirming.

I have experienced this momentum myself, and I bet you have as well—maybe you have even been the person who began it. You are in a group environment where someone took control of the situation by articulating a clear vision of the group's goals, an obvious passion for the work, and an ability to make the rest of the group feel confident and energized. There is your transformational leader. Transformational leaders are keenly aware of the importance of keeping lines of communication open so followers feel secure in sharing ideas and so leaders can directly recognize each team member's unique contributions.

Transformational leaders possess the characteristics of high energy: they are enthusiastic and deeply passionate. And not only are they concerned and hands-on in the process, but they have a team mindset, so everyone wins!

You know you are witnessing transformational leadership when you see leaders and followers encouraging each other to advance to a higher level of accountability and motivation. Because of their strong visions and personalities, transformational leaders can inspire followers to change perceptions, expand expectations, and motivate each other toward an aligned purpose.

Imagine for a minute how it would feel if your company were six times larger next year. Would that fit your growth plan? Would half of that growth be more than you could handle? Maybe such growth is impractical for your company, considering all you would have to do to support it. Without capitalizing on your progressive momentum, such results may be fleeting or unlikely. Know that you will make some mistakes and experience some failures, but if you keep momentum going, small setbacks will not keep you from moving forward.

WOMEN LEADERS

Speaking of transformational leaders, women can do a lot to transform your business and keep and even increase your company's momentum. While it is no secret that men dominate the corporate landscape, I believe women are more natural leaders. Leadership is influence, and influence is the result of one's ability to connect and interact with people. Women have that ability to a greater degree than men. I get a huge smile on my face when I reflect on women in leadership positions—Margaret Thatcher, Mother Teresa, Rosa Parks, and Eva Peron are just a few of the women whose leadership has changed our world in the past. Today's dynamic and inspiring female leaders include Danish Prime Minister Helle Thorning-Schmidt, Oprah Winfrey, Meg Whitman of eBay, Marissa Mayer of Yahoo, Christian speaker and author Joyce Meyer, and Navy Admiral Michelle Howard. These women have also changed many people's daily lives.

If you don't know some of these women, you should because they have some great insights. Another of the greatest women out there for many of us is known simply as Mom.

As a society, we need to do a better job of promoting, recognizing, and acknowledging the attributes that women possess and bring to the marketplace.

MISTAKES AND FAILURES

I have made a few mistakes in my career, and I expect to make a few more. If you don't have failures in your life, it's a sign that you just aren't trying hard enough to be great at something. When you make a lot of effort, some failure is inevitable!

Failure is typically the result of pushing the envelope. It happens to those who are trying to be *the best, fastest, and biggest achievers and creators* innovating today. Failure challenges you to make something positive out of it. It gives you a chance to tell a story about you or your company's adversity and how you bounced, healed, recharged, and conquered your way back to success. People can then identify with your story because they have their own challenges in their lives.

As you create new attractants for your company, you will be taking some chances. You may even be ridiculed at times for a questionable new process when you present it. Despite any naysayers, you *must* take the qualified and quantified chance. Call it opportunity. Call it vision. If you are not challenging yourself and others, how boring is that?

Life's real joy comes from putting yourself into a position where you could fail or succeed with one of your BHAGs (Big Hairy Audacious Goals). During such challenging times, you find out what you are really made of because you really have something on the line. Maybe you need to build a new office in a particular region before your competition does. Maybe you need to secure the next new team for your foray into the Midwest markets. Maybe you are simply looking to get a particular product to market first. You *might* fail, but what if you don't?

Searching for your internal catalyst as you head into failure allows you to discover a great strength in yourself that you probably didn't even realize was there. Even as you are assessing what got you to the point of failure, be cognizant that we all need a catalyst to get us back in the game. Sometimes that catalyst comes through other people's stories. It may even come from you as you bounce back after a failure. In most cases, I have seen people bounce back stronger, smarter, and more resilient than ever. They think, "If that last setback didn't kill me, I don't know what could. NEXT!"

The mistakes come when we continue to repeat the failures. If we are learning from our mistakes, then we are recognizing a pattern that we learn not to visit again. By discounting what you know doesn't work going forward, you quicken the pace on your road to future success. By the same turn, your teammates can benefit from you sharing those experiences so they don't have to contend with the same hurdles. Some examples of such mistakes to learn from might include misquoting something unintentionally, not getting back to a prospect within the expected time frame, or misfiring an onboarding schedule.

Sometimes you lose a prospect or client before you even have a chance to minimize damages. The saving grace in recovering from any mistake, unintentional as it may have been, is how you react immediately after realizing a mistake has been made.

You need to "own it!"

Deflecting or dismissing the mistake will immediately label you as not having integrity no matter how minor or major the mistake was. By not addressing the mistake, you are showing that you don't confront issues and you can't be trusted when people really need to count on you. Make apologies, but *never* make excuses.

Here are some examples of good apologies:

- "I am sorry I let you down. I should have gotten someone here to help you with your current job expectations. I know you are overwhelmed with the amount of production you are having to process. I did not check with the new person this past week to confirm she could be here today. I realize how this affects you personally, and I am sorry I didn't follow up better. Going forward, I will make a call on the Friday before someone's start date to validate her ETA."

- "I am sorry about the equipment not being here as promised so you could start on your project this week. I will do a better job of tracking ETAs in the future from our supplier. If it is okay with you, I have another training aspect we can start at this time to make good use of your precious time until we get your equipment."

Checking in with someone shortly after the incident to hold yourself accountable will be respected by the person involved and will get you back on the path of exhibiting high integrity in all you do. You may have to meet with someone again to reinforce your commitment to him or her of "always doing the right thing."

Remember, people will judge your sincerity not by what you say but what you do. Therein lies the truth of your intentions to make good on a mistake.

The sooner you own the mistake and address the issue with the affected party, the greater your opportunity to redeem yourself. Your client, prospect, or follower, believe it or not, has made some mistakes in life as well. We all have some moments we would like to have back to manage differently, so don't be too hard on yourself. Chances are that your competitors have messed up on the same point. Earlier, I related my story to you about my experience as president of a logging placement company early in my career and the hiring mistake I made.

Face to face is always the *best* means to express to someone your sincerity in wanting to get an issue out in the open and processed. Professionals do this on a regular basis, and they expect it of their counterparts. Be that guy/gal.

Request a meeting at your earliest convenience and set the expectation of resolving the issue then and there. Reassure the affected person that his perception of you and your company is everything to you and that you will strive to create and protect a relationship of mutual trust between you. The conversation should focus on how to avoid miscommunication in the future to maintain the positive relationship you are working so hard to nurture.

Equally, when you extend grace to someone who has just made a mistake, it can reap huge rewards. It is always best to give people the benefit of the doubt when coming across a mistake. I often meet with the person privately before addressing the issue in front of his peers and subordinates to avoid embarrassment for that person. Everyone is due professional courtesy.

I have been on the receiving end at times myself, and I have been appreciative of someone's discreet effort to save me from myself. Recently, I was about to speak at a Seattle City Council meeting on a hot topic to the council. I was informed beforehand that some constituents in the room would clearly be offended by the direction of part of my presentation. Fortunately, the person who informed me was more seasoned than I was on how to navigate through that kind of environment. Everyone always appreciates an opportunity to save face.

DON'T BE AFRAID OF MOMENTUM!

Anyone who's ever been on the threshold of a major success can tell you there is apprehension of the unknown. Those who have achieved great success become more comfortable with it and learn to manage the growth. We yearn for it, but we're also afraid of maximizing capacity. What if we start going too fast? What if we get out of control?

This is a great problem to have! Embrace it! Hire people to fulfill the service levels you are going to maintain. The biggest lesson is

"Don't be afraid." It is natural to hold back. When it comes to reaping your reward from your hard work, take it and keep moving.

This may be pointing out the obvious, but you have to believe in yourself. If you don't believe in yourself, who will? Detach from negative people to decrease the negativity in your life. When you are mindful of the naysayers and energy zappers, you can be grateful that you are not them. Seek out and surround yourself with positive people—not overly optimistic ones, but those who are supportive and look for the positive in every challenge.

By purchasing this book, I know you are trying to improve yourself. Grow your library of positive affirmations. Keep purchasing more education, enlightenment, and empowerment through all of the resources available to you. Turn to that library in times of self-doubt.

ENVISIONING

Some people are gifted with vision; they not only can imagine the future, but they can foresee it before others. This gift gives them a tremendous advantage not only within their companies but also their industries. If you have such people on your team, it can give you not only the whole picture but help you determine the pathway to reach it.

Nurturing the gift of vision in others also helps you to see the big picture. The vision fuels your great initiative and gives you the edge to embark on it before anyone else. The real benefit lies in using this gift not only to your advantage, but to the advantage of those around you. By sharing your vision, you bring your team along with you, and then everybody wins! If you as the leader cross the finish line first, you have missed a rich opportunity to build your team's trust and support. Finish together in stride and as a team—therein lies the joy. It is about the journey, not the destination.

As you perpetuate momentum and grow your team, the defining moments are those when you could have taken the glory for yourself, but instead, you made the correct choice to include those around you so everyone could participate in and benefit from the vision.

HARD WORK

> "My grandfather once told me that there were two kinds of people: those who do the work and those who take the credit. He told me to try to be in the first group; there was much less competition."

— **Indira Gandhi (1917-1984), Prime Minister of India**

There has never been a substitute for hard work. If you want the things that put you into a position of having more so you can do more, those things have to be earned.

All successful people work very hard. They also have a lot of fun working. Work is what they want to do. At the end of the day, work always exceeds talent. A lot of successful people will even admit to you that maybe they weren't the smartest or most talented, but they did outwork their competition. While some people are enjoying their advantage of having talent, the dogged, determined competitor is continually driving the platform that will let him prevail in the end. Personally, I wasn't the "A" student in high school or college; I didn't score the highest on tests, and I didn't attend a top notch university. But because I worked hard, today, a lot of the people who did have those accomplishments I have now contracted to work for me.

Many smart people don't achieve all of the success they deserve because they become satisfied with resting on their laurels. As a recruiter, it's important for you to know that. Don't assume possibly higher talent is motivated to challenge you and your recruiting efforts. While you continue to hone and improve your skills, the assumptive soul can be beat.

Continue to create the attractant and build a better me. Get really good at networking, prospecting, and social media engagement. The working smarter, not harder theory is a great one when you combine the smarts with the drive.

The people watching your company grow will be inspired by the efforts they see you putting forth and the pay-offs that result for you; watching you will teach them to be more focused with their time and maybe more efficient with their days. As for those who say, "I enjoy work; I could watch it all day," they will work out very well at your competitor's place of business.

With the momentum you are feeling right now, let's finish strong in the next chapter by "Putting It All Together."

CHALLENGE

When you have catapulted your momentum and strategy, what is next for you? Where do you go with your success now?

_____

_____

_____

_____

_____

CHAPTER 10

PUTTING IT ALL TOGETHER

"We are what we repeatedly do. Excellence,
then, is not an act, but a habit."

— **Aristotle**

First, let's review what you have learned so far about being a great recruiter and identifying the kind of culture you want to have as a result of your efforts:

- You have identified your culture
- You have created great attractants
- You are working on improving yourself
- You are executing on great networking activities
- You are prospecting with new tools
- You are making social media your friend
- You know how to cull the herd
- You know how to keep your prized team members
- You recognize and feel the momentum building
- You execute, execute, execute!

Do you believe your best days are ahead of you? They are!

Do you know there are people out there waiting for you to show up?

Keeping the right perspective is the key as you proceed toward your future success.

REFINING

As you continue to have success with your newfound recruiting prowess, keep in mind that you don't want to get stuck on a specific solution for improving your game. Recruiters often confuse the "What" (the problem they're trying to solve) of their business with the "How" (the preferred solution method). Moving from "What" to "How" happens so seamlessly that the process is almost automatic. Don't get stuck on the "How." Keep your eye on the "What," and treat the "How" as an option that may or may not be successful.

So how do you get to the "What"? Write out your current idea and ask yourself: "Why is this important? Does it serve our purpose? Is it aligned with our core values?"

Your answer to the "What" will give you the "How." You'll know that you are on the right path when some obvious answers appear that don't seem to have a lot of risk around them.

For instance, you have a new location you want to open in a market you are not currently in. The accountants, risk analysts, salespeople, and the demographics and logistics people all think it is a good idea. The new location is the "How." So what is the "What?"

If you move your thinking one level up, temporarily tabling the idea of the new location, and focusing on the realization that an obvious need exists for your product in that market because more and more customers there are requesting it, then you will realize that not having a presence there would be missing a great opportunity.

But does that mean that investing in a new location is the best solution? Would it pay to have more of a remote presence as opposed to a physical location? Could you subcontract to an entity already established in the area? Would your clients be better served by representatives traveling to the prospective location bi-weekly? How else could you address the problem?

Let's consider the example of an entrepreneur who wanted to create a live chat CRM tool for customer support on mobile apps. The live chat for mobile would be the "How." So what would be the "What"?

Tabling the initiative forces you to identify the core challenges and think creatively about all the ways a particular initiative can be addressed. What appears to be the obvious solution? Giving your team a chance to challenge itself from all perspectives—accounting, sales, administrative, and demographics—and test the prospective initiative will allow you to determine whether it's the best solution.

It is easy to get stuck in the "How." The "How" can usurp a lot of attention and distract you from the challenge you are hoping to address. So take the time to invest in the "What" before you invest in the "How." Don't be afraid to go for a different solution if the "What" calls for it. Removing that last layer of detail gives your business plan more wiggle room and allows you the room you need to make refinements down the road.

DISRUPTIVE INNOVATION

What is a disruptive innovation? Wikipedia defines it as:

> An innovation that helps create a new market and value network, and eventually disrupts an existing market and value network (over a few years or decades), displacing an earlier technology. The term is used in business and technology literature to describe innovations that improve a product or service in ways that the market does not expect, typically first by designing for a different set of consumers in a new market and later by lowering prices in the existing market.

Wikipedia itself is a disruptive innovation. Traditionally edited general encyclopedias have been displaced by Wikipedia, the free, non-profit, community-edited online encyclopedia. Former market leader *Encyclopedia Britannica* ended print production in 2012 after 244 years. Britannica's price of over $1,000, its physical size of dozens of volumes, its weight of over 100 pounds, and its update cycles lasting a year or longer were all annulled by Wikipedia. Wikipedia's lack of price, unlimited size, and instant updates are the primary challenges for profitable competition in the consumer market.

This book itself is a self-published book—a new innovation that is replacing the traditional book publishing business. There is a true paradigm shift occurring in the publishing industry. Super busy people will pay for someone to take care of the marketing and promotion of their book and there is still a need for that. For those of us who can or want to be more involved in the process, we now have options to consider. You have a 100 percent chance of your book getting to market when you self-publish, as opposed to a less than 1 percent chance of a publisher selecting your book; new technologies have made printing books less expensive, and by self-publishing, you keep all the profit rather than sharing your intellectual property and rights with a publisher. Yes, self-publishing is more work for the author, but you are in control of your destiny rather than relying on someone else to produce and promote your book.

If you think about it, disruptive innovations are occurring all around us. We have all watched the U.S. postal system losing market share to email. Newspapers continue to lose market share (advertising $$$) to video and social media. Even computers are losing sales to smartphones.

Ask yourself, "Where could I create a paradigm shift in my industry so I can attract more attention to my company for the best talent available out there?"

Do you create a mortgage environment that is totally online, intuitive, and offers an immediate approval that can close within a week? Do you create drones that deliver retail products directly to your home the same day you place the order? Do you create a process that streamlines healthcare insurance? Can you create a better system for finding great prospects for your company? Will you use some of the ideas you picked up in this book to make a paradigm shift at your company?

What is your "BHAG" (Big Hairy Audacious Goal) that you can get legs under and get others to support and grow?

Create an attractant that gets your industry's attention by disrupting its existing models for success. In the business world, we continually try to find what sets us apart from our competition. Recruiting is no different. Where you can gain an edge on your competition is by streamlining existing practices, skipping redundant processes, and improving efficiencies within your environment.

Disruptive innovators create and support an idea or initiative until others see the beauty in the innovation. You will know you have a successful innovation when others are feeling threatened by it. It may take years for the change to become "an overnight success," but suddenly, everything will have changed and brands that seemed to dominate will fall into a subordinate position.

A copycat of your innovation is a pale imitation of your company. Being first with an innovation sets you apart. A competitor that uses your innovation challenges your market share in a meaningful way and broadcasts your innovation. A concept, innovation, and business model can be mimicked—execution can't.

Be first. Be best. Be sure to execute!

REPLICATE

What brings you success today may not next year. Being aware of what brought you success and continuing to improve it is the key objective. Some current popular concepts will become antiquated within a short time frame. If you continue to improve "me," the natural growth cycle will perpetuate your success. So what do you need to do more of, and what do you need to do less of to maintain your success?

Once you determine the something you need to do more, make sure you harness enough time and energy to focus on it. The key is to ignite it without hesitation. The longer you deflect or get distracted, the longer it will take to meet your goal. Know when to STOP doing the things that keep you from what you need to do more of.

Here are five primary components that can serve as guidelines to assess and insure replication of your successes:

- **Objectives:** What were your objectives? Did you attain them? Was your business plan detailed, and did you follow it? Did the adjustments you made during the year enhance your objectives completely? Is there still some meat on the bone for that particular initiative?

- **Fiduciary Responsibilities:** Did you exceed your financial budget, or did you fail to spend the funds required to return even greater success? Why? Did you as a team get to the markers financially and by the date you forecasted? Was it the "why" that got you there? Is the same "why" in place for the upcoming year? If you did get a little behind monetarily this year, what did you do to catch up?

- **Team Support:** A successful objective usually requires success for the team as a whole. What was the best moment for the team this last year? To repeat that moment is TOUGH to do. But what led up to that great moment? That can be repeated. What was the glue that brought other departments into the alignment?

- **Markers:** Monitoring where you have been will give you a great indication of where you are going. A great business plan includes check-in points and accountability markers that expose your progress before you fall behind schedule. Did you measure weekly, monthly, or quarterly? Can you relax that schedule now, or is it time to make it more frequent? How did you decide what to monitor and when? Are there new markers to add, or are there some that should be eliminated?

- **Challenges:** Were you able to anticipate the learning curves? How did you overcome the learning curves (failures)? You will have new ones this year. Who managed those last year, and who will be managing those this year? Consistently moving through and forward on your challenges is the key to your long-term sustainability.

When you replace self-imposed negative limits with positive images that focus on your potential, your success is imminent. Eliminating self-limiting beliefs is possible so such beliefs need to be kept in check. Nail down specifics of what is creating doubt, such as: In which areas are we not having success recruiting? Next, define the area you are trying to recruit from. Ask yourself, "Are we favorably compensating our people at or above current compensation being received at the competition?" Once you have a set of facts and know your numbers (the basics), you can press the brand you have to offer to prospects.

EXPANSION

Be careful what you ask for. Expansion in some cases isn't for everyone. I have been involved in companies where we ran a lot more profitability when we were smaller than when we became larger with more headaches. For a lot of companies, expansion is mandatory for staying ahead of the competition and capturing the brightest talent out there. You wouldn't be reading this book if expansion wasn't on your mind. With some industries, you can reach a saturation point where the cost to expand just creates more expenses than what you will ever see in ROI (return on investment). Expansion is a tricky game. Expand too fast or too much and increased expenses and infrastructure pressure can be taxing. Expand too late and your business could get passed up by the competition.

Some tipping points will let you know the business is outgrowing you or the business model has gotten you to the present place in time and space. The business reaches a point where you and the current crew can no longer manage all the work. As the leader, you recognize you need help. Maybe it's a larger space, better equipment, a missing sales force in an opportune area. These tipping points are mandating that you take control of the company's future. As you start to manage this transition, recruitment is again paramount to success. Tipping points are a great problem to have. Rejoice in them!

With expansion comes more responsibility. Your existing employees may now be overwhelmed by the new load of responsibilities. It's time to get clear about new job descriptions and expectations and recruit. Respect the people who got you to this point and cross-train them, making them more valuable to your company.

Depending on your industry, you may need more delivery people, another person or two in accounting, five or six more salespeople, a couple of IT gals, a group for R&D, a COO, and a CHO (Chief Happiness Officer)....

Communication is critical in so many areas, and during expansion, it is key to keep your people informed of "*What* is next," "*Where* we are headed" and "*Why* we are doing what we are doing."

Communicate, communicate, communicate through virtual meetings, face-to-face meetings, email, YouTube videos, telephone calls, team huddles, the company Facebook page, and anything and everything you can use to get the word to everyone with a transparent and clear message about the "What," "Where," and "Why" of your expansion.

Your loyal and longer term employees will have confidence in the expansion message you send to them based on your past history of communicating. If good communication isn't part of your past history, you are going to find high anxiety and mistrust coming from your people. Communicating well and often gives you another chance to do it well and correct past mistakes.

Here are some issues I have experienced in the past when expansion was in play:

- Our surveys show more and more people are not satisfied with our services. We rely on those surveys as a barometer for how we are doing. If customers are leaving empty-handed or going to our competition because we are "too busy," we have to change that or succumb to the competition, which may be doing it better. I want you to keep your jobs and our company strong.

- We have asked too much of our valued employees and we see people experiencing "burnout." We are making more and more mistakes, missing deadlines, and falling short of customers' expectations. The leadership team is recruiting additional talent to complement our current hardworking team. Thank you for your diligence and positive attitude in this time of expansion; it will eventually benefit all of us.

- Our figures show that our competition is expanding operations in areas we haven't been able to reach. If we as a team aren't taking aggressive action toward giving customers easier access, we may all end up working for ABC Company.

- Our business and industry is affected by many factors, including the very industry we are in. In the mortgage business, we are inundated with new guidelines and government regulations. We all know what has been going on with the healthcare industry, and look at what has happened with the automobile industry. The new technologies improving our daily lives are changing daily. That creates a new dynamic that causes overnight adjustments. Our company and you need to stay in step if not be ahead of the "next big thing."

Expansion requirements that are out of our control. Remember 911? Think of all the changes that occurred overnight for the airline industry, the import/export business, the communications industry, travel, economic policies, the military, and in politics. Some things we just don't see coming, but we need to be prepared for anything.

Expansion is fun and invigorating. You are being rewarded for your efforts. You've gained more market share, received more requests for your product, created more of a need to service your clients fully, and now require more people in more space. The expansion will require attention to detail by you and your team. Enjoy your success and manage it well.

ONCE SUCCESS HAPPENS

Now that you have gotten your company noticed and people are seeking you and your company out, you have beat the competition for top talent. You have culled the herd and done it well. You've trained your strong team members. You are retaining the people you have worked so hard to get. We have all heard the saying "Strike while the iron is hot." You have done so and built a successful rhythm.

Continue to be patient, prepare, and plant seeds. You are about to be rewarded for your efforts.

This is where it becomes a HOOT!

It is time to stop dreaming, you are in the zone. Now implement the following with the machine you are building:

- **Show people you care about them and their success.** The best thing you can do to build endearing loyalty from your prized employees is to be transparent.

- **Include your people in your company's vision on a regular basis.** Encourage them to share their ideas on how to improve. Repeat the vision so the *team* feels it is part of a bigger thing.

- **Practice the little things.** For example, make it a point to stop by each employee's desk or workplace and just say, "Hi." Such little things are a big deal to your employees. Even your existing employees appreciate that. It is especially important to stop by to greet new hires and express how happy you are to see them at the company. Doing so immediately makes people feel welcome, and it gets a positive relationship on the fast track to teamwork and camaraderie.

- **Create new opportunities for your peeps.** Most of the top people you hire came to you because there was promise and an opportunity to grow in their chosen field. It is up to you to allow an individual to stretch in new directions. The best people don't want to be confined to static job descriptions. Work on evolving positions frequently. People who grow and gain more knowledge in your industry have a broader perspective and a deeper understanding of your company culture, creative sales strategies, and marketing tactics. They can leverage that knowledge across the company and across the industry.

- **Don't be afraid of feedback:** Ask your employees for a report card and *act* on it. My company continually sends out surveys to clients to ask, "How are we doing?" By the same token, we shouldn't be afraid to ask our employees for feedback. It does expose us to vulnerabilities and reflects on us and our management team, but better you know how your employees feel and grow from it than continue down the wrong road. Embrace and face the changes that need to be made to create an environment where all are focused on the betterment of the whole.

The goal here is to recognize when we are reaching the tipping point—the point where your company has created a significant attractant in your industry.

As Steve Jobs told Stanford University's graduating class in 2005, "Stay hungry and stay foolish."

NEVER FORGET WHAT MADE YOU GREAT!

Never forget what made you great. For larger companies especially, one of the biggest mistakes continually repeated is forgetting to do the little things that made them great. Instead of having your prospects meet your HR department first, ask your leaders/department heads to reach out directly to them. Everyone is busy, but I bet that last bad hire cost you more money than you would have possibly spent by deeply getting to know a prospect through a little more conversation or vetting of prospect's personality profile and past employment relationships.

Are you still making a habit of personally engaging the people who work with and for you on a regularly scheduled basis? They do want and need to see you.

Do you know what their families are involved in? Are you still having socials in and outside of the office? Do you let your hair down and come from a place of humbleness, or are you entertaining being pompous and cavalier with your new title? Are you staying approachable and genuine in your interactions with not only your superiors but your friends and subordinates who got you where you are today? Those people will continue your momentum or be the cause of your ineffectiveness going forward.

Don't lose the culture that originally attracted people to your company. The business environment changes, but it's just like riding a bike. You may get a newer bike with different bells and whistles that goes faster, but remember that you started riding it to get you somewhere. The idea is to get back to basics, even when the scenery changes and new markets emerge. Remind yourself what the basics were that first got you to the place of opportunity and abundance. Maintain your ability to listen well, instead of reacting fast, and identify root causes, instead of just treating symptoms.

MAINTAIN YOUR BUSINESS CHARISMA

Most people want to be liked and, in turn, want their companies to be liked. You know you do. As recruiters, we are continually seeking ways to validate ourselves and fulfill this desire to be recognized and liked.

If you are gifted with charisma and can apply it to your business, you will have the magic element for sustainability. In any competitive business situation, having charisma will make you more likely to gain trust, develop relationships, and win the business.

Did you know that we make decisions emotionally and justify them logically? It makes recruiting fun to know that we can influence an emotional decision that happens subconsciously. I know that decisions can be influenced. I know that the qualities of a likeable person can be cultivated and proactively developed in the business world. Staying calm and collected under pressure is one trait that makes people charismatic. The same goal can be achieved with a business' culture.

One technique I have learned and put into play over the years is "mirroring." Mirroring is copying the other person's physical mannerisms, movements, and facial expressions when engaged in a conversation. You become a mirror image of the other person.

In Stephen Ministry, I was trained on how to mirror someone. For this particular exercise, we would break up into groups of three, and the first person was responsible for recalling a particular emotional experience he had in his life. The second person was assigned the task of imitating facial expressions, reactions, and body language as the first person shared his experience. The third person was to mimic and refine the emotions based on his observations from the second person until the third person felt the second person had it down exact.

When the exercise ended, we did a recap. The second person explained what she was feeling and was very in tune with what the first person was feeling and was even aware of a deeper understanding of the first person.

Another simple example might be when you are interviewing someone and you see him cross his legs and point them toward you (a sign of engagement), and then you reply in a like manner. If the person points his legs to the door (a bad sign), it's not a great time to mirror.

Mirroring is an excellent, time-proven way to gain a quick relationship with another person! In addition to mirroring someone's body language, it also helps to speak in a similar tone (tonality). Speak at the pitch the other person is engaging you with unless he is agitated over something. Always engage someone with a comfortable level of eye contact. Keep in mind that you are, in effect, having a social "dance" in which the people involved fall in step with one another in a manner that is in unison and unforced. Again, there is a fine line between mimicking and mirroring. Be sure not to mimic the other person. But do match his arm movements with small hand gestures and his body movements by your head movements; this is called cross-over mirroring, and it is highly effective without being noticeable in a way that can be interpreted as offensive.

Now that you are conscious of mirroring and aware of its effects, you can use it as a tool for generating chemistry and effective alignment during communication. The next time you're engaged in a conversation with someone, try mirroring body language, posture, and facial expressions. You will find that the conversation suddenly feels very friendly and open. Repeat back to someone, "What I think I heard you say was…?" Rephrase or paraphrase her words to make sure you really understand what she was saying. Think of this technique as verbal mirroring. By asking questions about someone's interests or feelings, you are mirroring her interest in herself.

Earlier in the book, I mentioned that nothing is sweeter than someone hearing his or her name. Aren't you impressed when someone you only met one time or just recently remembers your name? Since birth, our parents, teachers, friends, and family, have acknowledged you with the sound of your name in your brain. Your name captures your attention instantly. It makes you feel important and respected, filling your desire for attention and love.

Can you remember the last time someone you just met ended the conversation by stating, "Nice to meet you, (fill in your name)?" Didn't you feel acknowledged? Someone was actually interested in you enough to remember your name, and you want to return the favor.

Here are some great name association techniques I have employed that have helped me:

Observe a person and choose a "marker." What is the first thing you notice about a person? You are looking for something on his or her face or head that is permanent. Hairstyle, makeup, and glasses can change by the next time you see someone. Don't "mark" temporary "markers" on a person. Examples might be large ears, eyes, nose, birthmark, scar, teeth, dimples, chin, etc.

Associations for large ears might be: Bob Radar, Jerry Receptor, Sue Hearing, Betty Volume, Gary Flight, Mabel Lobes, or Bart Opie.

Some associations for eyes might be: Jim Blue, Carrie Snake, Barney Round, Sheila Brown, Marcie Green, William Sleepy, Tammy Close, Tabitha Engage, or Marty Wide.

Some birthmark associations might be: Rhonda Roads, David Blemish, Brenda Reds, Walt Cheek, Greg Mole, Marna Chin, or Valerie Lake.

Don't be thinking about what you are going to say next. Pay attention to the person's name as it is given. This is your only opportunity to get it right. As you hear the person's name, repeat it out loud. Use his or her name in your conversation and for sure when you are saying goodbye to the person.

I also use association in another way through rhyming or picture association. For instance:

- Abby..."A" bee
- Blanche...Branch
- Caesar...Salad

- Darren…Dare/Run
- Emily…Family
- Frank…Hot Dog
- Garrett…Gear It
- Howie…Mandel
- JoAnna…Mobanna
- Maxine…Magazine
- Tammy…Tame/Me
- Violet…Flower

Obviously, use whatever works best for you. I just want to open your mind to some simple techniques that work.

CELEBRATE

Throughout this book, I have consistently urged you to celebrate your achievements; don't live there, but always celebrate when milestones, goals, or deadlines have been met. One of the driving reasons for our existence as human beings is to find joy in life and to bring joy to those we love and know.

Make it memorable and make it fun. Here are some things I have done in the past to celebrate:

- **An evening at the horse racetrack.** Charter a bus or buses and be singing the *Gilligan's Island* theme song or traditional Irish songs on the way to the venue. As people get off the bus, hand each person $100 to bet on the horses. Cap it off with a nice dinner and more songs on the way home.

- **Sponsor a dinner at a dueling piano show.** Everyone gets involved and people can request the songs they love.

- **A harbor cruise**. Add a band and a magician onboard. Can you tell I am from Seattle?

- **Hire a flash mob.** Flash mobs delight everyone and transform the everyday through an extraordinary and inspiring surprise. Hiring a flash mob corporate production company is an affordable way to leave a lasting impression on your company and clients. Tie one in to month-end celebrations, marketing campaigns, product launches, grand openings, conferences, association meetings, holiday parties, galas, awards events, press announcements, client events, and whatever!

- **Outdoor Segway treasure hunts**. The two-wheeled personal motorized vehicle can be great fun for your current employees to find items of value placed around town. Invite prospective employees to participate as well.

- **Speed painting.** Do it in overhauls, shorts, Elton John Glasses, in '50s garb, alternative dress, unmatched shoes and socks....

- **Cook a formal dinner for your peeps**. *You* do it! I mean *you* organize it and date it; *you* cook the meal. *You* set the table. *You* present the dishes and embellishments to be served, and *they* clean it all up! Depending on the size of your group, you may need some slight assistance getting the meal to the table and setting up, but *you* should do most of the dinner on formal tableware. Remember, *gratitude* and *celebration* can be combined. It is a lot of work, but it is fulfilling and rewarding, and it comes directly from *you*.

- **An afternoon at the movies**. Include lunch for you and your clients with the film. Some cities don't have the private movie venue, but the ones who do take advantage of it. It's a great return for your money.

- **Celebrate Cinco De Mayo.** Have people bring their own Mexican dishes. I don't care if you are not Hispanic. The timing might be such that it aligns with an initiative you have just completed. Keep your peeps guessing what is next!

In this book's introduction, I made the statement that no companies last forever. There have been some pretty impressive standouts through time. *Business Today* (November 29, 2011) reported that Kongo Gumi, a construction company out of Japan, had been around since the year 578. It was the world's oldest continuously ongoing independent company, operating for over 1,400 years until it was absorbed as a subsidiary of larger construction company. The company fell on hard times and liquidated in January 2006. Kongo Gumi's assets were purchased by the Takamatsu Corporation. Before its liquidation, the company had over 100 employees.

One of the older companies in the United States today is the DuPont® Chemical Company, founded in July, 1802. It originally started as a gunpowder mill by Éleuthère Irénée du Pont. Over the years, it has had to refocus its mission and change with the times to stay in business. Today, the company's recruiting focus is on the global challenges ahead for us as a species and how we can solve global challenges together. The company speaks of how the future will be one of inclusive innovation, so together we can feed the world and build a secure energy future. Which age group do you think this recruiting style appeals to the most?

Lastly, what about your bucket list items? Don't forget a happy heart equals a happy home. Are you taking the time to get the things you want out of life—the things you are literally working for so you can have them? What things do you feel would challenge you that you want to pursue, or what would you be curious to see whether you could accomplish? Save up your money, educate yourself, and initiate something you want to do at least once in your life that will be worth every penny and every minute spent preparing for it.

CHALLENGE

You have had a series of challenges assigned to you throughout the previous chapters. Have you been sincere in your efforts to improve your recruiting skill set? I want you to be better at what we do on a daily basis in the recruiting world. If at this point I haven't moved you to take some corrective actions to enhance your recruiting efforts, then I have missed the mark in terms of this book's whole objective. This is the accountability tipping point for me and for you. Please consolidate the "best" ideas that you know you can implement effectively and jot them down below. Make them your daily affirmations.

FINAL NOTE:

WHAT A HOOT! LET'S RECRUIT!

"Knowledge is power."

— **Francis Bacon**

Execution and implementation are the common denominators that set apart those who achieve from those who fall short. I purposely gave you a "Challenge" at the end of each chapter so you could start implementing immediately while ideas were fresh in your head.

The road to success is littered with people who had good intentions. You have invested your precious time in reading *What a Hoot! Let's Recruit!* to find some tips to make you better than who you were before you read it.

You are responsible for taking advantage of some new learned skill sets that most people know they should but just won't implement. Here is where you set yourself apart from those who think these techniques are a good idea and then watch you do it. Never let limiting beliefs leave you finding satisfaction in an excuse.

I hope this book has inspired you to discover further the natural strengths that you already possess and some new strengths you may not have even known you possessed. If you find yourself wandering from time to time, refer back to the "Challenge" sections that asked you to reflect on some of the ideas rolling around in your head; with a little effort, you can put those ideas to use in a positive way to achieve the kind of success you seek.

We have to commit to new behaviors a number of times before they finally become habits. Habits then become second nature. Can you commit to making permanent changes that will not only benefit you but those around you by becoming more effective in everything you do?

What are the Top Ten things you promise to yourself and an accountability partner to do within the next ninety days that will hold you to implement your newly acquired recruiting skills? Successful people always write down their goals (promises to themselves) so they can conceptualize the order, progress, and finish line for each project they embark on. This is not a suggestion. This is a must do for you. Please stop and do that now.

So...you have learned to create attractants. You have learned how to prospect in a more effective way. You have learned how to use social media effectively. You now know how to retain your valuable people and how to sustain synergy and momentum when you are in the zone. And if you need a refresher on any of those areas, now you have *What a Hoot! Let's Recruit!* to refer back to. I encourage you to reread and mark this book up; bend the pages and use it as a tool to keep you on track for the work that needs to be done.

If there is a concept you need more clarity around, please let me know. If you have captured a whale (stellar recruit or recruits), I want to hear from you. Tell me what you liked about this book and what you didn't like. I will give you a complimentary 30-60 minute consultation to discuss your challenges. My phone number is (425) 344 2066. My email is jjensen@hootinrecruiting.com

I wish you much good luck on this journey you are embarking on. You will find it exhausting at times, yet invigorating with a newfound energy, to know you are on a path to accomplish what others continue to struggle with. Remember that we never get *there*. When we get the present project accomplished, it makes us aware of a bigger picture that spurs us into another level of accomplishment. Having many options is the key to continual growth and larger opportunities.

I appreciate that you spent your hard-earned money to purchase *What a Hoot! Let's Recruit!* What will bring me the most joy is that you use it and share some of your wins with me.

To your success,

Jeff Jensen

ABOUT THE AUTHOR

Jeff Jensen started his recruiting career in 1982 at the age of twenty-six as CEO/President of the Knapp Agency, a management and secretarial placement firm in downtown Seattle. After a few years of recruiting successfully for regional as well as national firms, he sold the Knapp Agency and took the opportunity to become President of the Lynnwood Placement Center, which placed logging personnel in the Northwest as well as Southeast Alaska. This was an exceptional experience for Jeff and taught him early on how a "bad hire" can quite literally cost lives. With issues like the spotted owl and environmental protection laws becoming stricter, the need for companies to call on the Lynnwood Placement Center for personnel began to dry up. Time for change....

Jeff loves to embrace change and the growth that comes along with it. Some of the principles Jeff refers to in *What a Hoot! Let's Recruit!* are patterns of leadership style, balancing family and work, personal and group achievement, and creating the essential mindset needed to prosper no matter what the state of the economy, business, or things beyond your control.

The last twenty-plus years of Jeff's experience have been related to the mortgage industry. In that time, he has been an executive vice president for Golf Savings Bank, a principal at Homestead Mortgage, a branch sales manager for First Horizon Home Loans, and a branch sales manager for Aspire Lending. All of those positions have required recruiting to be a part of Jeff's job description, and during this time, he has confirmed that in both great and not-so-great markets, consistent time-proven strategies and techniques will prevail.

Jeff is currently a director of the Washington State Mortgage Lenders Association. He is also past president for the Seattle Mortgage Bankers Association; during his presidency, in 2011, membership grew by 32 percent in what many would call a down year for the industry.

Jeff recently grew a branch from eight to twenty-eight employees in a one-year period in 2011—a 71 percent increase in a down year.

With over thirty years of recruiting experience, Jeff has become very successful with growing companies and capturing great talent while enduring the variations that are the new normal for many companies.

Jeff's passion for recruiting has come from seeing some really great people benefit from being placed at the right companies, thereby allowing them to be more than they ever thought they could be. His attitude of servanthood and passion for helping others achieve their goals and aspirations in their lives, careers, and businesses has created lifetime friendships and extraordinary results. Jeff is thankful and full of gratitude for the people he has assisted with time-tested and proven systems that work.

Jeff was born in Wichita, Kansas, and he moved to the Seattle area when he was twelve years old. He and his wife Taryn have been married thirty-eight years and live in Woodinville, Washington. They are the proud parents of three young men: Jason, Landon, and Brady.

BOOK JEFF JENSEN
TO SPEAK AT YOUR NEXT EVENT

If you are in charge of choosing a professional speaker for your next event and you are looking for maximum benefit while being vibrantly engaged in a topic that can set your company apart from the competition, then Jeff Jensen is your speaker.

Jeff will leave your audience or colleagues with a new zest for recruiting that will make a major difference in your company or association's growth.

Whether your audience is a mid-size or large company or association, you will find the techniques that Jeff Jensen shares to be not only useful but life-changing.

Jeff Jensen can present a positive and customized message geared toward alignment with your organization's culture and initiatives. At the same time, he will motivate your group to achieve things they weren't aware were possible. His stories are filled with inspiration, achievement, and everyday scenarios that will help people adjust in a positive way to events that change people's lives.

In the thirty years Jeff Jensen has been in the business of recruiting, he has acquired a unique set of experiences that he brings to the audience in a colorful way. Jeff makes a habit of engaging his audience with stories from the audience members as well as experiences they can share for all to benefit from.

Jeff Jensen's purpose when he speaks is to bring humor, entertainment, and inspiration to your group that will assist it in achieving extraordinary results in the challenge we call recruiting.

If you are looking for a memorable speaker who will leave your group wanting more and ask to have him back again and again, book Jeff Jensen today.

You may contact Jeff Jensen directly to schedule a complimentary pre-speech interview by phone at (425) 344-2066.

You can also visit the *What A Hoot! Let's Recruit!* website at: www.hootinrecruiting.com or contact Jeff by email at jjensen@hootinrecruiting.com